THE

LIFE OF JESUS CHRIST

FOR THE YOUNG

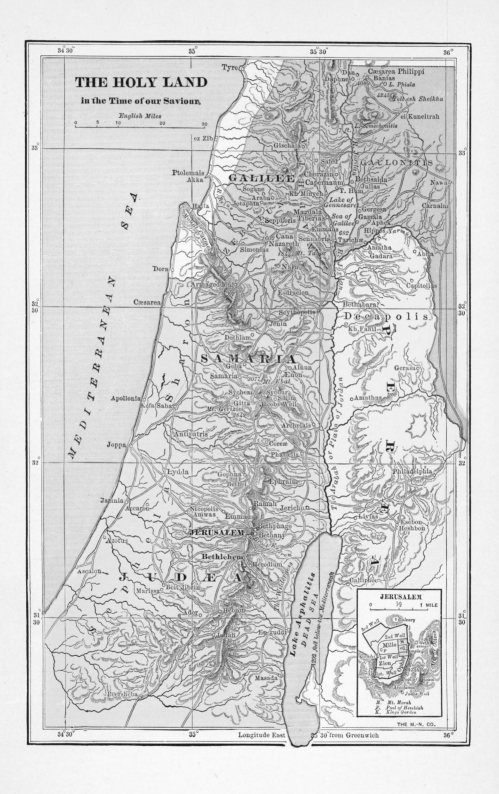

THE HOLY LAND
in the Time of our Saviour.

English Miles

0   5   10   20   30

Tyre

Dan
Daphne
Cæsarea Philippi
Banias
L. Phiala
4245
Tell esh Sheikha
el Kuneitrah
L. Semechonitis

ez Zib

Gischala

Safed

Ptolemais
Akka

GALILEE

GAULONITIS

Nawa

Chorazin
Capernaum
T. Hum
Bethsaida
Julias

Haifa

Sogane
Araba
Jotapata
Kh Minyeh

Carnaim

Lake of
Gennesaret

Magdala
Sepphoris Tiberias

Gergesa
Gamala
Aphek

Cana
Nazareth
Emmaus
682

Sea of
Galilee

Hippos Yarmuk

Simonias

Sennabris
Taricha

Amatha
Gadara

Abila

Mt. Tabor

Dora

Nain

Cæsarea

Armageddon

Esdraelon

Capitolias

Bethabara?

MEDITERRANEAN SEA

Scythopolis

Decapolis

Jenin

Kh. Fahil

Dothiam

Apollonia

SAMARIA

Geba
Ainun
Enun

Gerasa

Samaria
Mt. Ebal

Sychem
Sychar
Salim
Jacobs Well

Amathus

Kefa Saba

Gitta
Mt. Gerizim

Antipatris

Joppa

Coreæ

Phasælis

PEREA

Lydda

Gophna
Bethel

Ephraim

Philadelphia

Jamnia

Nicopolis
Amwas

Ramah

Jericho

Livias

Accaron

Emmaus

Bethphage

Azotus

JERUSALEM

Bethany

Esebon
Heshbon

Ascalon

Bethlehem

Herodium

Callirhoe

JUDÆA

Marissa
Beit Jibrin

DEAD SEA

Ador

Hebron

En-gedi

Judah

Masada

Beer-sheba

Lake Asphaltitis

JERUSALEM

0   ½   1 MILE

M. Mt. Morah
P. Pool of Hezekiah
K. Kings Garden

Longitude East from Greenwich

THE M.N. CO.

THE

LIFE OF JESUS CHRIST

FOR THE YOUNG

BY THE

REV. RICHARD NEWTON, D.D.

AND

HIS LIFE DEPICTED IN A
GALLERY OF EIGHTY PAINTINGS

BY

WILLIAM HOLE
ROYAL SCOTTISH ACADEMY

VOL. I

PHILADELPHIA

GEORGE BARRIE'S SONS, Publishers

Dedication

TO

CHRISTIAN PARENTS, MINISTERS, TEACHERS

AND ALL WHO ARE

Striving to Follow the Command

OF

OUR BLESSED LORD TO HIS APOSTLE PETER

"FEED MY LAMBS"

THIS WORK IS

Most Respectfully Dedicated

BY THEIR FRIEND AND FELLOW LABORER

THE AUTHOR

CONTENTS

VOLUME I

THE GALLERY OF THE LIFE OF JESUS CHRIST

—

VOLUME I

The Angel Gabriel and the Virgin Mary

And in the sixth month the angel Gabriel was sent from God unto a city of Galilee, named Nazareth. To a virgin espoused to a man whose name was Joseph, of the house of David; and the virgin's name *was* Mary. And the angel came in unto her, and said, Hail, *thou that art* highly favored, the Lord *is* with thee: blessed *art* thou among women. And when she saw *him*, she was troubled at his saying, and cast in her mind what manner of salutation this should be. And the angel said unto her, Fear not, Mary: for thou hast found favor with God. And Mary said, Behold the handmaid of the Lord; be it unto me according to thy word. And the angel departed from her.—*St. Luke i: 26–30, 38.*

NOTE BY THE ARTIST

The Virgin Mary is here represented in the ordinary attire of a woman of the country, kneeling in prayer upon the mat or carpet, which, laid upon the floor, serves the purposes of a bed.

1

THE FIRST PROMISE

GOD tells us in the third chapter of Genesis, and the fifteenth verse, what the first promise is; it says: "I will put enmity between thee and the woman, and between thy seed, and her seed; it shall bruise thy head, and thou shalt bruise his heel."

These words were spoken about six thousand years ago. They carry us back to the Garden of Eden. That was the place where God put Adam and Eve to live after they were created. What a beautiful place it must have been! God had made to grow there "every tree that was pleasant to the sight, and good for food." The loveliest flowers too were blooming there. No thorns nor briers were growing in that garden.

The birds sang sweetly among its shady groves. Nothing disagreeable, or hurtful, or poisonous was to be found there. The animals were all tame. They played lovingly with each

1

other, as we sometimes see the young lambs playing together in the meadow. How bright and beautiful every thing must have been in that charming place! Well might it be said that "God saw every thing that he had made, and, behold, it was *very good.*"   Gen. i: 31.

And the reason why every thing was so bright and beautiful and happy in that garden was that there was no sin there.

We know not how long Adam and Eve continued to enjoy the happiness of that blessed place.   But, we know that by and by a change came over them and their beautiful home.   For after awhile we are told that Satan stole into the garden.   Taking the form of a serpent, he tempted our first parents to break the only commandment that God had given them. They yielded to Satan's temptation.   They broke God's law.   This was the first great sin committed in our world.   This was what we call the fall of Adam—or of man.   The effect of that one sin was terrible.   It was like putting poison into a fountain, and making all the streams that flow out from it poisonous too. Adam and Eve became sinners, and the consequence of this was that all their children also became sinners.

As we think about this, it seems as if we were standing and looking at the brightness and beauty of that garden, and while we are looking the whole scene changes. A heavy cloud arises. It spreads all over the sky. It turns the day to night. It shuts out every ray of light, and leaves those two poor sinners trembling in the dark.

And now God comes down to speak to them about what they have done. They are terribly frightened, and try to hide themselves. But there is no hiding from him. No wonder Adam and Eve were afraid. They had good reason to fear. They knew they had sinned against God, and displeased him. They could not tell what he was going to do with them. He had told them before that if they ate of the tree which he had told them not to eat of—"*in the day that they did so, they should surely die.*" But they had never seen any one die. They did not know what death meant.

Now we remember that Adam and Eve had each a soul, as well as a body. The soul can die as surely as the body. And the soul can die while the body is still living. The souls of our first parents, according to God's word, did die in the day when they sinned by eating the forbidden fruit. And afterwards when they had children, these were all born with dead souls. And this is what the apostle Paul means when he speaks of people as being "dead in trespasses and sins," when they are born into the world. Ephes. ii: 1. We are all born with dead souls. And so it was true in this sense as God told our first parents, that, "in the day they sinned they *did* surely die."

They probably expected that their bodies would die too. And so they stood trembling to hear what God would say to them, or to find out what he was going to do to them. There were three persons before God when this meeting took place in the Garden of Eden. Adam and Eve were there and Satan too, in the form of a serpent. God spoke to them separately, and told what the effect of sin would be upon each of them. What he said to the serpent we read in Gen. iii: 14. What he said to Eve we see in verse 16, and what he said to Adam we read in verses 17-19. But still, up to this point God had not told Adam and Eve what he was going to do with them and their children. They did not know whether he was going to have mercy on them and help them, or whether he would leave them to die in their sins. But before he went away from them, on that first meeting after they had sinned, God was pleased to say something to them on this point. What this was we find in Gen. iii: 15. "I will put enmity between thee and the woman, and between thy seed, and her seed; and it shall bruise thy head, and thou shalt bruise his heel."

This is called "*the first promise.*" It is the very first thing in the Bible that points us to Jesus. It showed Adam and Eve that God was not going to leave them in their sins, but that he intended in some way or other to show mercy to them and their children. This must have been a great comfort to them. It must have seemed to them just as if the dark storm-cloud, which sin had brought over their sky, had opened above them, and one bright and beautiful star of hope had come shining out upon their darkness. Everything that the Bible tells us afterwards about Jesus was wrapped up in this first promise.

This is the one spring out of which the whole stream of God's mercy to us flows forth. You know what a fine large stream the river Rhine is—as it flows through certain parts of Europe. And yet far up near the top of one of the high mountains of Switzerland, there is a tiny little spring, which a man can span with his hand—I spanned it with my own hand in going over that mountain—and yet, that little spring is the source or fountain from which flows forth the great river Rhine. And so this first promise is the spring from which the river of God's mercy and salvation, for our whole world, flows forth.

We cannot tell how much Adam and Eve understood about this first promise. We know a great deal more about it than they did. For we have the whole Bible to help us understand it. And we come now to talk about this first promise in the light which the rest of the Bible throws upon it. "I will put enmity between thee and the woman, and between thy seed and her seed; it shall bruise thy head, and thou shalt bruise his heel." And when we come to look at this verse, in the light of the Bible, we can see in it the promise of four things.

In the first place we can see here the promise of a helper.

The part of the verse which shows us this is that in which God says:—"I will put enmity between thee and the woman." The word "thee" here refers to Satan. And here perhaps some one may say,—"Well, but I don't see any promise of a helper here." Perhaps you do not at first; but let us talk about it a little and I think you will soon see it. Now remember what Satan had just done with Adam and Eve. He had persuaded them to give up having God for their Lord and Master, and to take him instead of God. When they did this they gave themselves up to Satan and put themselves in his power.

Let us take an illustration of what we are now speaking about. Suppose we compare the soul of Adam to a fort, or palace. When God created him good, and put him in the Garden of Eden, then that fort belonged to God, with all the goods that were in it. It was God's fort, and God's flag was flying on the walls of it. Satan wanted to conquer that fort, and get possession of it for himself. He knew that God, the owner of this fort, was stronger than he was, and so he did not try to storm the fort or take it by violence. He saw that there was only one way in which he could succeed, and that was by deceit and treachery. He could not batter down the walls of the fort, or force open the gates. So he came to Adam and Eve, and told them lies about God, and tried to persuade them to open the gates of the fort, and let him in. And this was just what they did when they broke God's law, and obeyed Satan rather than God. They opened the gates of the fort to him, and let him in. He took possession of it as his own. He hauled down God's flag from the walls of the fort, and ran up his own flag in the place of it. Then the fort was his, and he expected to remain the owner of it, and of all that belonged to it forever. He supposed that Adam and his children would always be on his side, and that there never would be any more enmity or fighting between them. And if God had not intended to send us a helper, it would have been as Satan supposed. He would have always kept the fort. His flag would always have waved over its walls, and we should all have been left forever in his power.

But God showed that it was not to be so, when he said to Satan—"I will put enmity between thee and the woman." This meant that he would not let Satan keep the fort he had taken by treachery, but that he was going to take it away from him. It was just as if God had said to Adam and Eve, and to all their children; "Satan has gained a great victory over you, but don't be discouraged. Don't give up to him, for I am going to help you." When

God said he would put enmity between Satan and the woman, it was just as if he had signalled to our first parents in the language of the popular hymn, saying—

" Hold the fort, for I am coming."

They could not "hold" the whole "fort," but they might get a little corner of it, and hold on to that till they could see what God was going to do for them. And so, in this "first promise," or in these words spoken in the Garden of Eden, one thing that we find is the promise of a helper.

And then in this first promise we find *what sort of a helper this was to be.* He was to be a— HUMAN—*helper.*

We are told it was the *"the seed of the woman"* who was to be this helper. "The seed of the woman" meant some one who was to be born of the woman, or of our mother Eve. It meant one of her children, or descendants. The apostle Paul settles this point, by telling us positively that this "seed of the woman" refers to Jesus Christ, our Saviour. Gal. iii: 16.

I suppose that if God had not said that the helper he was going to send was to be one of Eve's children—a human helper—a man—it would have been most natural for Adam and Eve to have expected this promised helper would have been an angel. No doubt the angels from heaven had often visited our first parents while they were in Paradise. They had talked with them freely, and had told them a great many things about God,—about how he had made the world, and about other matters which they would be very glad to know. They knew how much wiser, and stronger, and better the angels were than themselves, and it would have seemed reasonable for them to have expected that the helper promised to them would be an angel. But when God said that this helper was to come as "the seed of the woman," then he taught them that he was to be a man—a human helper. It is supposed by some people that when Cain was born—the first child Eve had— she thought that he was to be the promised helper: for she said to Adam then, "I have gotten a man, or *the* man from the Lord." Gen. iv: 1. If this was so, she made a great mistake, for the helper promised here did not come till four thousand years after that. How sadly she must have felt this mistake when called to mourn in the bitterness of her sorrow over the death of Abel!

It is a great mercy to us that Jesus, our helper, is a man, and not an angel. If he were an angel he would not know how to help us: he could not feel for us, and sympathize with us, as he does now. The angels were never born children as we were. They never grew up to be boys and girls as we did. They could not tell how boys and girls feel, and what troubles they have to bear. And this is one reason why people— even good people—have always felt afraid of angels when they have appeared to them. If Jesus our helper, had been an angel, we who are children, could not go to him, as we do now, and speak to him, in the words of that sweet hymn:

"Thou, who once on mother's knee,
Wert a little one like me,
When I wake or go to bed,
Lay thy hand upon my head;
Let me feel thee very near,
Jesus Christ, our Saviour dear.

"Once thou wert in cradle laid,
Baby bright, in manger shade,
With the oxen, and the cows,
And the lambs outside the house;
Now thou art above the sky,
Thou canst hear thy children cry."

The first thing that children do, when they get into any trouble is to run to their mother, and tell her about it. And they do this because they are sure that she will feel sorry for them, and help them. Jesus knows this, because he is a human helper. And so, in one of his precious promises, he says—"As one whom his *mother comforteth so will I comfort you.*" Is. lxvi: 13.

And the apostle Paul tells us that this was one reason why Jesus took our nature upon him, and was born of a woman. In coming to be our helper, he came as a human helper, rather than in any other way, because then he could tell all about our feelings, and would know best how to help us in our troubles. Heb. ii: 14-18.

Suppose you break your arm. When the doctor comes in to set the broken bone, and put on the splinters and bandages, it will give you a great deal of pain. And if while you are suffering this pain, a friend, who has had a broken arm, comes in, and sits down by your side, and says—"I am very sorry for you. I know just how you feel, for I remember very well how I felt when my arm was broken;" you would find more comfort in the sympathy of that friend, than if he had never known what it was to have a broken arm.

Visit of Mary to Elisabeth

And Mary arose in those days, and went into the hill country with haste, into a city of Juda. And entered into the house of Zacharias, and saluted Elisabeth. And Mary said, My soul doth magnify the Lord. And my spirit hath rejoiced in God my Saviour. For he hath regarded the low estate of his handmaiden: for, behold, from henceforth all generations shall call me blessed. For he that is mighty hath done to me great things; and holy *is* his name. And his mercy *is* on them that fear him from generation to generation. He hath shewed strength with his arm; he hath scattered the proud in the imagination of their hearts. He hath put down the mighty from *their* seats, and exalted them of low degree. He hath filled the hungry with good things; and the rich he hath sent empty away. He hath holpen his servant Israel, in remembrance of *his* mercy. As he spake to our fathers, to Abraham, and to his seed for ever. And Mary abode with her about three months, and returned to her own house.—*St. Luke i: 39, 40, 46–56.*

NOTE BY THE ARTIST

The difference of costume worn by women of Northern and Southern Palestine is distinctly marked. The Virgin wears the holiday dress of a Nazarene; Elisabeth that of a woman of Bethlehem and its neighborhood.

2

One of the celebrated kings of England was Henry the Eighth—the father of the queens Elizabeth and Mary. The story is told of him that he used sometimes to disguise himself, so that no one would know who he was. Then he would go about to different places in London, so that he might see what was going on, in a way that he could not do if he should go there openly known as the king. On one of those occasions he got into some trouble, and was taken up by the police. They had no idea that their prisoner was the king, or else they would have released him in a moment. But he would not tell them who he was. And so the policemen put him in the common prison, and locked up there he had to spend the night. It was a cold, dark place, very different from his comfortable palace, and the unknown king suffered a good deal during that long dreary night.

The next morning they let him go, and he went off. On getting back to his palace, one of the first things he did was to send a sum of money to the keeper of the prison where he had spent the night. This money was to be used in furnishing fire and lights, for the benefit of those who might have to be locked in that prison all night.

Now this dark world of ours must have seemed like a dreary prison to Jesus, our blessed helper, when he was living here.   And as King Henry, on getting back to his palace, remembered how cold and dark the prison was, where he had been shut up all night, so Jesus our helper, in yonder glorious home where he now lives, never forgets how his people feel, and what they need to comfort them while they are living in this dark world of sin and sorrow.   And so we see that when this "first promise" tells us about the helper who was to come to us through "the seed of the woman," it is a *human* helper to whom it refers.

And then the third thing about this helper of which this promise tells us is—that he was to be a—SUFFERING—*helper.*

We are taught this when we find God saying to Satan, about the promised helper of men, "*thou shalt bruise his heel.*"   We all know that the heel is not a very tender part of our bodies. And yet we know that if a person has to walk about, and work with a wound in his heel it may cause him a great deal of suffering.   And when we are told here that Jesus, our promised helper, was to do his work for us with a bruised heel, we are taught that his work was to be done through suffering.

"*Thou shalt bruise his heel.*" If we wish to know what this means, we cannot get a better explanation of it than is found in the fifty-third chapter of Isaiah. There we see how it is that Jesus Christ, our promised helper, was to suffer for us, and was to do us good by his sufferings. There he is spoken of as "a man of sorrows and acquainted with grief." There we are told that "he bore our griefs and carried our sorrows." There it is said that "he was wounded for our transgressions, and *bruised* for our iniquities." Here we see how the very word which God made use of in the first promise is applied to Christ. There it was said "thou shalt *bruise* his heel;" and here Isaiah says—"he was *bruised* for our iniquities."

If we look at the suffering life that our Saviour led while here on earth and then remember what a hand Satan had in causing those sufferings, we shall see how well it might be said that all through the days of Christ's ministry in our world Satan was bruising his heel. Jesus was suffering through all those forty days in which he was led up into the wilderness "*to be tempted of the devil.*" Then it might be said that Satan was "bruising his heel." Jesus was suffering when the Jews found fault with him, and called him hard names; when they said he "was a Samaritan, and had a devil," and that he did his mighty works "through Beelzebub, the prince of the devils." It was Satan who stirred up the Jews to do these wicked things to Jesus, and so in this way he was bruising his heel. And in the Garden of Gethsemane we know what terrible sufferings Jesus passed through. There he said "my soul is exceeding sorrowful even unto death." There "being in an agony he fell to the earth, and his sweat was as it were great drops of blood falling down to the ground." And then he was dragged before Pilate and charged with crimes he had never committed; he was mocked, and scourged, and crowned with thorns, and spitted on. He was smitten on the face; he was struck on the head with the reed. He was nailed to the cross, and lingered for long hours there in terrible suffering. And when we know that Satan was the leader in all these trials through which Jesus had to pass, how well it might be said of him then that he "was bruising the heel" of Jesus.

I am very sure that Satan did not know what great good was to come out of the sufferings that he caused Jesus to pass through, or else he never would have brought them on him.

I suppose that Adam and Eve understood very little of what was meant by this bruising the heel of the promised helper. But we know what Jesus suffered for. We understand why it was that his heel was bruised. You, and I, and all of us have a great interest in it. *Jesus was helping us when he let his heel be bruised.* He was suffering for us, he was bearing the punishment of our sins. He was our substitute. And a substitute, you know, is one who suffers in the place of another. And here is a story to illustrate the good that follows to us from the sufferings of Christ, or the bruising of our helper's heel. It occurred in the experience of school life, and is told by the teacher, in whose school it took place. It is called—"The Little Substitute."

"Several years ago," says this person, "while I was teaching a school, one of the boys broke the rules of the school. The punishment for his offence, according to the law of the school, was for the offending boy to stand in the corner of the room, in disgrace for a quarter of an hour, and then to receive a whipping. I called him up and told him to go to the place of punishment.

"As he was going, a little boy, younger than he, came to me and asked that he might take the place of the guilty one. I wondered at this and spoke to him about the disgrace, and the punishment he would have to bear. But still he begged that he might go. I consented, and he went and took his companion's place in the corner.

"I was greatly surprised and affected, but thought I could teach the boys a good lesson from this incident.

"The little boy stood out the quarter of an hour, and then bore the flogging like a hero.

"When it was all over I inquired whether the other boy had asked him to take his place.

"'No, sir,' he replied.

"'Don't you think he deserved to be punished?'

"'Oh! yes,' said he; 'he deserved it well.'

"'Then why did you wish to bear the punishment in his place?'

"'Sir, it is because I love him.'

"This filled my eyes with tears. All the school had listened with great interest to this conversation. I then called George—the boy who had been disobedient—and ordered him to go stand in the corner, and receive the punishment himself. In a moment a multitude of voices cried out at once:

"'Oh! sir, that wouldn't be right; that wouldn't be right.'

"'It wouldn't be just either,' said one of the larger boys.

"'Why wouldn't it be right?' I asked, thinking to puzzle this boy. 'Hasn't George broken the rules of the school?'

"'Yes, sir; but you have allowed Joseph to be punished in his place, and now you ought not, on any account, to punish George.'

"'Well, my dear boys,' I continued, 'does what has just happened recall anything to your minds?'

"'Yes, sir,' said several of them, 'it reminds us how the Lord Jesus Christ bore the punishment of our sins.'

"'What name would you give to Joseph for what he has now done?'

"'The name of *substitute*,' was the answer.

"'And what is a substitute?'

"'One who takes the place of another.'

"'And whose place has Jesus taken?'

"'Our place, as sinners,'" was the answer.

And so when we read how "the heel" of Jesus was "bruised," we see that he was a *suffering helper;* and how he helped, or saved us, by his sufferings.

The last thing that we learn from this promise about our helper is that he would be—A SUCCESSFUL —*helper.*

God taught us this when he said to Satan— "*it shall bruise thy head.*" The "it" here means "the seed of the woman," or the helper promised to us—or our Saviour Jesus. Satan was to bruise the heel of Jesus; that means he was to cause him a great deal of suffering. But then, on the other hand, Jesus was to bruise the head of Satan, or of the serpent. The head of a serpent is the most tender part of his whole body. Some animals, as the bear for instance, are so strong in the head, that it is hard to hurt them by hitting them there. But if you wish to kill a serpent you strike it on the head. But when it is said that Jesus, our promised helper, was to "bruise the head" of Satan or the serpent, it does not mean that he was to kill him.

There is a verse in the Epistle to the Hebrews which may help us to understand this part of the first promise. It is in the second chapter and the fourteenth verse, where the apostle Paul is speaking about Jesus our Saviour; and he says that "*by his death he was to destroy him that had the power of death, that is the devil,*" or as he is here called "the serpent."

Now there are two ways in which we may speak of a person as being destroyed. One of these is when he is killed. Another is when the power he has had to do harm is taken away. But when we are told that Jesus, our promised helper, was to "bruise the serpent's head," or to destroy him, it does not mean that he was to kill him outright, but that he was to destroy, or take away his power to tempt men, and lead them into sin.

Let us take an illustration here from the history of our own times. Some years ago you know, the famous Napoleon Bonaparte was the Emperor of France. He was a great soldier; his greatest delight was to be at the head of large armies; to lead them into battle, and to gain great victories. In his many wars he caused the death of hundreds of thousands of men. It seemed as if there could be no settled peace among the nations of Europe while he was in the midst of them. War followed war just as the waves of the sea roll in after each other. But at last the Duke of Wellington, at the head of the English army, gained a great victory over Napoleon at the battle of Waterloo. Napoleon's army was scattered. He himself had to flee. He was taken prisoner, and confined as a captive on the little island of St. Helena, in the midst of the Atlantic Ocean. In that battle Napoleon lost his empire. That event is always spoken of as the downfall, or the overthrow of Napoleon. And we are in the habit of saying that the Duke of Wellington *destroyed* Napoleon. If it were right to apply the language of scripture to such an event we might say that he bruised Napoleon's head when he gained that great victory over him. This does not mean that he killed him, or destroyed his life. It only means that he took away his dominion, or destroyed his power.

And this is what Jesus, our great helper, does to Satan. When the first promise said that he was to bruise Satan's head, it did not mean that he was to kill him or destroy his life; but it meant that it was to take away his dominion, or to destroy his power. And Jesus does this in two ways. One way in which Jesus "bruises the head" of Satan is *by converting souls, and delivering them from Satan's power.*

Until we are converted, and become Christians, we are the prisoners or captives of Satan. The Bible says—"*we are taken captive by him at his will.*" II. Tim. ii: 26. Every unconverted soul is like a fort which Satan has taken possession of, and which he holds in his own power. When that soul is converted, then it is taken away from Satan. His power over it is destroyed. It is handed over to Jesus, and his dominion is established there. This is what the apostle Paul means when he speaks of those who are converted, and become Christians, and says— *"they are delivered from the power of darkness, and are translated into the kingdom of God's dear Son."* Col. i: 13. And so, everytime that Jesus converts a sinner, and makes him a Christian, it may well be said that he is striking a blow at Satan. He is bruising his head, or destroying his power.

We may take the apostle Paul as our illustration here. He was a very learned man. His mind was uncommonly clear and strong. But before his conversion all his learning and ability were employed in the service of Satan. He had that great man completely in his power. Satan made him, as Paul afterward said—"a persecutor and a blasphemer," and one who was very "injurious" to the cause of the gospel. He did all he could to destroy the followers of Jesus. He imprisoned them, and put them to death. Paul's soul was like a strong fort on the side of Satan. It was altogether in his power.

But when Paul became a Christian, what a wonderful change took place! He began at once to preach that very gospel which before he had been laboring to destroy. He went all up and down the world telling about Jesus and his wondrous grace and love. He became the greatest preacher that ever lived. Multitudes of people were converted by him. He established churches wherever he went. He wrote thirteen out of the twenty epistles which the New Testament contains. His writings have been a blessing to the church and to the world for eighteen hundred years. And here we see how Jesus bruised Satan's head, or destroyed his power, when he converted Paul's soul. And he does the same, in some degree, every time that a soul is converted. This is one of the ways in which the first promise is fulfilled, and Jesus, "the seed of the woman, bruises the serpent's head."

But there is another way in which the promise will be fulfilled, and Jesus will bruise Satan's head, and this will be by *delivering the world* from his power. He has not done this yet; but he certainly will do it by and by. This is what the apostle Paul means when he says—"The God of peace *shall bruise Satan under your feet shortly."* Rom. xvi: 20. Satan is now called "the God of the world," II. Cor. iv: 4, and the "prince of the power of the air." Ephes. ii: 2. But the Bible tells us that the time is coming when Satan will be driven out of the world. We read (Rev. xx: 1-3) how a mighty angel will come down from heaven, and bind Satan in chains, and lock him in the bottomless pit. Then he will be a prisoner or captive, and his power will be destroyed, just as Napoleon Bonaparte's was when he was made a captive in the lonely island of St. Helena. Then Satan will not tempt, or deceive men any more. This will be a blessed world then. There will be no wicked people in it. Nobody will be cross or ill-tempered. There will be no swearers or liars. Nobody will cheat then. There will be no robbers or murderers then. No prisons or penitentiaries will be needed in those happy days. "Then men will beat their swords into plowshares, and their spears into pruning hooks, and they will learn war no more." Then "the leopard shall lie down with the kid; and the calf, and the young lion, and the fatling together; and a little child shall lead them." Then "the people shall be all righteous;" "and they shall not hurt, nor destroy, saith the

Lord, in all my holy mountain." And when this "good time comes," and all the world is as bright, as beautiful, and as happy as the Garden of Eden was before sin entered there, then this first promise will be fulfilled; and we shall see how clearly Jesus spoken of in this first promise has been *a helper—a human* helper—*a suffering* helper—and *a successful* helper. All the work that Jesus was to do for us, and for our world was wrapped up in these wonderful words —"I will put enmity between thee and the woman; and between thy seed and her seed; it shall bruise thy head, and thou shalt bruise his heel."

Joseph and Mary Arrive at Bethlehem

And Joseph also went up from Galilee, out of the city of Nazareth, into Judea, unto the city of David, which is called Bethlehem; (because he was of the house and lineage of David.) To enrol himself with Mary his espoused wife. And so it was, that, while they were there, the days were accomplished that she should be delivered. And she brought forth her first-born son, and wrapped him in swaddling clothes, and laid him in a manger; because there was no room for them in the inn.—*St. Luke ii: 4–7.*

NOTE BY THE ARTIST

A Syrian Khan or Inn is wholly devoid of privacy. Shallow and unfurnished recesses, open for the most part, and but slightly raised above the level of the ground, provide the sole accommodation for travellers, whose animals with their attendants are crowded together in the central area.

3

NOAH'S ARK

IF we look at a beautiful landscape in summer-
time from a hill-top, we often see dark
shadows moving slowly over the fields. And
then if we look from the fields below to the sky
above, we see where those shadows come from.
Great masses of white, fleecy clouds are floating
through the sky. It is those clouds which make
the shadows we see moving over the fields. And
if we look carefully at one of these moving
shadows we can find out a good deal about the
cloud that makes it. We can tell whether it is
a big cloud or a little one. We can tell whether
it is round in its shape, and smooth in its edges,
or whether it is rough in its edges, and irregular
in its shape.

In the same way, if we are walking away from
the sun, when it is setting in the western sky,
we can see our own shadow cast upon the road
before us. If we stand still, and some one draws

the outline of our shadow on the ground that person, even if he had never seen us, would be able, from examining the shadow, to tell whether it was made by a person large or small, by a man or woman, a boy or a girl.

Now, the Bible, God's blessed book, is like such a landscape spread out around us. And when we come to read the Old Testament, we find many things in it that appear to us very much like shadows we often see in summer, moving over the fields as we gaze on them. The apostle Paul tells us of these Old Testament stories that they "were written for our learning." Rom. xv: 4. And in another place he says they are "*a shadow* of heavenly things." Heb. viii: 5. They are—"*a shadow* of things to come, but the body is Christ." Col. ii: 17. He means by this that the principal persons whose histories we read in the Old Testament, and the leading events and incidents recorded there, were intended to teach us about the work that Jesus was to do for us when he should come into the world to be our Saviour. And now, I ask you to come with me, and let us take a good long ramble together through the field of the Old Testament, to study some of the shadows which are there, and try to learn what important lessons they teach us about Jesus.

The first of these, selected for our present subject is—"The Ark of Noah."

This is the earliest shadow of Christ that we find in the Bible. And when we come to examine this shadow, and draw as it were its outline, we see *four* things in it which seem to point to Jesus, and teach us very important lessons concerning him. We may begin by speaking of the—*size*—of the ark.

Noah, who built the ark, lived more than four thousand years ago. That was only a little over sixteen hundred years after Adam was created, and men began to live on the earth. But, in that comparatively short time, the people in the world had become very wicked. Noah and his family were the only persons in all the world who feared God. In consequence of their wickedness God had made up his mind to destroy every living creature in the world, except Noah and his family. And he determined to do this by bringing the deluge, or flood of water, on the earth. The object God had in view in doing this was to check the growth of wickedness, and teach men the dreadful nature of sin.

But, before doing this, God told Noah of his purpose. At the same time he gave him directions about an ark or vessel which he was to build, and in which he and his family were to be saved, while all the rest of the world was to be destroyed by the waters of the flood. The family of Noah consisted of eight persons. These were Noah and his wife, with his three sons and their wives. These eight persons were the only human beings, out of all the multitudes of people then living, who were to find shelter and safety in the ark. But, in addition to himself and his family, Noah was to take with him some of the birds of the air, of the cattle of the field, of the beasts of the forests, and of the creeping things of the earth, in order to keep them alive, and that they might fill the earth again when the flood was over.

What God said to Noah about this we read in Gen. vi: 19, 20. "And of every living thing of all flesh, two of every kind shalt thou bring into the ark, to keep them alive with thee, they shall be male and female. Of fowls after their kind, and of cattle after their kind, of every creeping thing of the earth after his kind, two of every sort shall come unto thee to keep them alive." A larger number of certain kinds of birds and animals were to be taken in. For in Gen. vii: 2, 3, we read—"Of every clean beast thou shalt take to thee by sevens, the male and his female; and of beasts that are not clean by twos, the male and his female. Of fowls also of the air by sevens, the male and his female, to keep seed alive upon the face of the earth." The animals called clean here were such as were offered in sacrifice to God. The unclean birds and animals were those which were not allowed to be thus used.

We are not told, and therefore we do not know, how many different kinds of birds and beasts and insects were taken into the ark with Noah. But God just knew how many of them there would be, when he gave directions to Noah how large he was to make the ark. He never makes a mistake in doing anything. You know we have a number of oceans on our earth. There is the Atlantic Ocean, and the Pacific Ocean, and the Indian Ocean, and so on. And when God made these oceans he knew exactly how much water was to be put into each of them, for the Bible tells us that "He measured the waters in the hollow of his hand." Is. xl: 12. And so he knew how large to make the basin, or bed, which was to hold the water of each of the oceans. And in every case he has made it of the proper size. And God is quite as careful in making little things as he is in making big things. Here is a baby; look now at the baby's eyes. Each of them is a little ball—a wonderful ball, indeed,—not quite round, but rather longer one way than it is the other. And each eye has a little hole, or socket, as it is called, made for it, in the bony part of the baby's head. God has made millions on millions of eyes. And each of these has had a socket exactly fitted for it. The socket for each of your eyes, and each of my eyes, just fits it. It is neither too large nor too small. God does all things well. "His work is perfect." Deut. xxxii: 4. And so when God told Noah about the size of the ark—its length—its width—you may be sure that he knew exactly how large it ought to be in order to have room enough for all who were to be sheltered in it from the coming flood.

This was the measure after which it was to be made:—The length of it three hundred cubits, the breadth fifty cubits, and the height thirty cubits. We are not quite certain how much a cubit was, according to our measure. It is generally supposed that is was eighteen inches, or a foot and a half. Then, according to this measure, the length of the ark was four hundred and fifty feet, its breadth seventy-five feet, and its height forty-five feet. It was not intended for fast sailing, but for safe floating, and so it probably had not a sharpened bow and a rounded stern as our ships have. We may think of it as a great square wooden house, six times as long as it was broad. The square or block of a city street is generally about five hundred feet long, and sixty feet wide. An ordinary three-story house is about forty-five feet high. So we may think of the ark as a floating house, or vessel, nearly as long as one of our squares, half as wide again, and about as high as a three-story dwelling.

We may be sure, therefore, that it was large enough for the purpose for which it was intended. And so when Noah had finished the ark he carefully stowed away all the food for those who were to live in it for so long a time. And when every thing was ready the birds of the air came flying to the window of the ark. The cattle came,—horses, and cows, and camels, and sheep, and asses. And the wild beasts of the forest came,—the bears, and the lions, and the tigers, and the elephants. Noah did not

have to seek them, neither did he muzzle or
chain them, for God took away their fierceness,
and even the lions were gentle as lambs. What
a strange sight it must have been! See, there
are those wild animals losing their fear of man,
and moving along as quietly as we sometimes
see the cows walking home from the pasture,
when the milking time has come. Noah put
them in the places he had prepared, and found
there was room for them all. The ark was large
enough to take in every living thing for which
it was prepared.

And when we think of the size of the ark, we
see how this shadow points us to Jesus. When
he was in our world he said, "Come unto me
all ye that labor and are heavy laden, and I will
give you rest." Matt. xi: 28. Many burdened
souls came to him then. And ever since then
they have been coming to him. They are
coming to him still. Let them come,

> "Yes! whosoever will,
> O, let him freely come;
> And freely drink the stream of life,
> 'Tis Jesus bids him come."

Jesus is the true Ark, of which Noah's ark
was only the type or shadow. And as *that* ark
was large enough to take in all for whom it was

intended, so is *this* Ark. No matter how many millions have already come to Jesus, "*yet there is room.*" In every land, in every age, for all who feel their need of him, and who are willing to come, there is a warm welcome, and an abundance of room.

We may alter one word in the hymn we often sing, and say there is,

> " Room in the arms of Jesus,
> Room on his gentle breast,
> There by his love o'ershaded
> Sweetly our souls may rest."

And so when we think of the *size* of the ark we see how this shadow points us to Jesus.

In the next place when we think of the—SUPPLIES —*with which the ark was furnished,* we see another thing about this shadow in which it points to Christ.

We have seen already that the ark was to carry large numbers of living creatures. They were all to stay in the ark for about a year. A great quantity of food would be required for them, and a great variety. In the places where those different creatures have lived they had always found the food they needed prepared for them. God is so good that he provides for the wants of all the creatures he has made. This is

what David teaches us, when he looks up to
God, and says,—"Thou openest thine hand, and
satisfiest the desire of every living thing." Ps.
cxlv: 16. What a beautiful thought this is! It
represents all living creatures in this world,—
the birds of the air, the beasts of the field and
the forest, and the creeping things of the earth,
as making up a great family. God is in the
midst of them as the Father of it. He holds in
his almighty hand all the good things that any
of his creatures may need for their life and comfort. And as he opens his bountiful hand, the
wants of every member of his great family are
supplied.

But when Noah had finished the ark there
was no food for the animals who were to make
their home within it for a year. God might
have fed them by miracle every day. But he
never works a miracle when it is not necessary.
It was not necessary here. So God told Noah
to take food enough into the ark for all the
animals. In Gen. vi: 21 he said to him,—"Take
thou unto thee of all food that is eaten, and thou
shalt gather it to thee; and it shall be for food
for thee, and for them." What a strange list
Noah must have had to make of the provisions
that would be needed for that long voyage, not

round the world, but *over* the world! No doubt
God helped him to make that list, and told him
what he was to take.

Nothing was overlooked, nothing forgotten.
The ark was filled and all were in their places.
The door was shut. The fountains of the great
deep were broken up, and the ark went floating
over a drowning world. Every living thing in
the ark found the food that was needed to keep
it alive and make it comfortable.

And here the ark was a shadow that points us
to Jesus. It teaches us this great and precious
truth, that when we come to Jesus as our friend
and Saviour, we are sure to find all that we can
need in him. David taught us this truth when
he said,—"They that seek the Lord *shall not
want any good thing.*" Ps. xxxiv: 10. Our
Saviour himself taught the same thing when he
said,—"Seek ye first the kingdom of God, and
his righteousness, and *all these things*"—that is
food, and raiment, and every thing necessary—
"*shall be added unto you.*" Matt. vi: 33. And
this was what St. Paul taught us when he said,
—"My God shall *supply all your need* according
to his riches in glory by Christ Jesus." Phil.
iv: 19. And what Jesus does for his people
now, and has always been doing for them, in

supplying all their wants, was beautifully taught in a shadowy kind of way by the ark, when we are told how well it was furnished with an abundance of all things that the health and comfort of its numerous passengers would require.

Now let us look at the way in which those who are loving and serving Jesus always find him ready to help them, and to do for them whatever they really need.

"Answers to Prayer."—The Rev. Newman Hall, of Surrey Chapel, London, gives this instance of answer to prayer. It occurred in his own experience. The superintendent of his Sunday-school felt a strong desire, one Saturday evening, to call on a member of his Bible-class, to inquire if he needed anything. He had never visited him before, and could not account for the desire he felt to do so then. He found his young friend very ill. The mother and sister seemed to be in very comfortable circumstances; but still he ventured to ask them if he could help them in any way. They burst into tears, and said that the sick young man—their son and brother—had been asking for food, and they had none to give him. When the teacher knocked at the door *they were both on their knees, asking God to send them the help they so much needed.* Their difficulty was met at once, and so the promise was fulfilled in which God says, —"And it shall come to pass, that before they call, I will answer; and *while they are yet speaking, I will hear.*" Isaiah lxv: 24.

Here is another illustration of the same kind: —A poor widow was very anxious about her rent, which she had no money to pay. She was sitting thinking what was to be done, when she heard a low voice coming from the next room mingled with sobs. She went to the door and listened. It was her little son George, who had lately given his heart to Jesus, and become a Christian. He was thanking God for giving him such a dear, good mother. Then he told the Lord how much his mother was distressed because she had no money to pay her rent; and then he finished his prayer in this simple way:— "O, Lord, pay mother's rent. Please do for Jesus' sake. Amen."

She said nothing, but went away. The next day a lady came, who had heard of her troubles, and gave her money enough to pay her rent.

"Everything in Jesus."—A Christian lady was in the habit of visiting some poor colored people, reading the Bible to them, and trying to lead them to Jesus.   Among them was a poor old woman, whose mind seemed as dark as her skin.   "When I talked to her about Jesus," says the lady, "she used to say, 'It's no use, Missus, I nebber can find him.   De Lord Jesus, don't want dis poor ole darkey.'"

"But one day when I opened her door her face was so bright that I knew she had 'found him.'

"Well, auntie," I said, "you feel better to-day, don't you?"

"'Oh! yes, honey, bress your heart, chile! I've found him.   Jesus dun come to dis ole darkey sinner.   I *doesn't want nuffin now.*'   Here was a poor old creature with nothing in the world to call her own; without food or clothing, but what was given her in charity, yet feeling that she was made 'rich in Christ Jesus.'   'I'se found Jesus, and *doesn't want nuffin now.*'   She felt that she had '*every thing in Jesus.*'"   And when we think of the ark, with its plentiful supply for the wants of all on board, we see how, in this respect, it was a shadow pointing to Jesus.

But let us take another look at the ark, and when we see how all who entered it found—SAFETY —*in it*, we see another thing in which it was a shadow, or type of Christ.

Announcement of the Birth

And there were in the same country shepherds abiding in the field, keeping watch over their flock by night. And, lo, the angel of the Lord came upon them, and the glory of the Lord shone round about them: and they were sore afraid. And the angel said unto them, Fear not: for, behold, I bring you good tidings of great joy, which shall be to all people. For unto you is born this day in the city of David a Saviour, which is Christ the Lord. And this *shall be* a sign unto you; Ye shall find the babe wrapped in swaddling clothes, lying in a manger. And suddenly there was with the angel a multitude of the heavenly host praising God, and saying, Glory to God in the highest, and on earth peace, good will toward men.—*St. Luke ii: 8—14.*

NOTE BY THE ARTIST

Herding sheep was considered by the Jews to be amongst the humblest of occupations; it was assigned, therefore, to bondmen chiefly, and to younger sons.

4

It was a long and dangerous voyage which the ark was to make. It had to go floating on its way, over a flood of water that was sent to drown a wicked world. Outside of the ark we are told that nothing was left alive. Gen. vii: 21, 22. We can easily understand what great dangers must have surrounded the ark while all this was going on. The rain came pouring steadily down without interruption for forty days and forty nights. How heavy this rain was we may imagine when it is said, that "the windows of heaven were opened." Gen. vii: 11. How swollen the rivers must have been! and how wildly their waters must have gone sweeping over their banks and rushing over the land! And in addition to this we are told that "the fountains of the great deep were broken up." Gen. vii: 11. The meaning of this seems to be, that the waters of the great oceans broke loose from their appointed beds and went roaring and surging over the earth. What a fearful time that must have been! How wildly those rising floods must have swept all before them! And when to the sound of those mighty waters there was added the loud roaring of the terrified beasts and cattle, and the wild cries and shrieks of the drowning multitudes, we can form some faint idea of the alarming dangers that must have surrounded the ark. And yet no accident happened to it. It went floating steadily over those heaving and troubled waters, and all within it were in peace and safety. No evil came to one of its many passengers. The Lord God Almighty spread his wings over it to protect it. He kept that ark and all it contained in the hollow of his hand, and so they all found safety there. They passed through that long voyage without injury of any kind. And when the storm was over, and the waters had gone back to their place, the dry land of the renewed earth appeared. And then as the inmates of the ark came out into the bright sunshine once more, and the rainbow of God's promise was seen stretching its beautiful arch over them it seems as if every man, and woman, and beast, and bird, and creeping thing as they went forth rejoicing must have been ready to say, either by word, look or action, "we found *safety* in the ark."

And what a beautiful shadow the ark was of Jesus in this respect! All who flee to him for refuge find safety. He says himself,—"Look unto me, all ye ends of the earth, and be ye *saved.*" Isaiah xlv: 22. It is surprising how much is said in the Bible about salvation, but it is always spoken of as "the salvation which is in Christ Jesus." 2. Tim. ii: 10. He is called "the God of our salvation." Ps. lxv: 5,—"the *captain* of our salvation,"—Heb. ii: 10,—"the *author* of eternal salvation." Heb. 5: 9. As the ark carried Noah and his family through the dangers of the flood, and landed them safely on the shores of the renewed earth, so Jesus—our Ark—will carry all his people through the storms and dangers of this life, and land them safely on the shores of the heavenly world.

At the close of his life in this world, Jesus said to his Father in heaven,—"Those that Thou gavest me I have kept; and none of them is lost." John xvii: 12. And of all his people he says,—"My sheep shall never perish, neither shall any pluck them out of my hands." John x: 28. It was not the wooden ark, but Jesus in the ark that saved Noah from the dangers of the flood. He saved Jonah when he was far down in the depths of the sea. He saved Daniel in the den of lions, and his three friends from the burning, fiery furnace. And the apostle Paul assures us that "He is *able to save unto the uttermost*, all that come unto God through him." Heb. vii: 25.

It is surprising how much the Bible says about the safety of those who come to Jesus as their ark. In one place he is spoken of as "the eternal God," who makes himself a "refuge" for his people, and puts underneath them his "everlasting arms." And then it is said,—"The beloved of the Lord"—this is the tender and affectionate way in which Jesus speaks of his people—"The beloved of the Lord shall dwell in *safety* by him." Deut. xxxiii: 27, 28. We all know how well the eye is protected in its place in the head. The moment anything dangerous comes near it, the lid shuts down upon it, and it is safe. And Jesus uses this as an illustration of the safety that his people find in him. He says that he will keep them as safely as the apple of the eye is kept. Deut. xxxii: 10. In another place he says that if anybody touches one of his people he will feel it as quickly as we should if a person attempted to touch that most tender of all parts of the body—the eye. Zech. ii: 8. Suppose you have a precious jewel, which you are afraid of losing, and which you wish to keep in perfect safety. You open your hand. You put your jewel in the palm of your hand, and then shut it up. How safe it is there! And Jesus uses *this* as an illustration of the safety which his people shall find in him. He promises to keep them in the shadow, or the hollow of his hand. Is. xlix: 2. But even if you held that jewel in the palm of your hand, it would not be perfectly safe there. Some one stronger that you might appear and compel you to open your hand, and take your jewel from you. Or if this should not take place, by and by, you might get tired and fall asleep. Then your hand would open, and your jewel might drop out. But when Jesus holds us in his almighty hand neither of these things can happen to us. None can make him loose his hold on us. And then he never grows weary, never slumbers, or sleeps; and so those whom he holds in the hollow of his hand find *perfect safety* there. And thus, when we remember how safely the ark carried all who were in it through the dangers of the deluge, we see what a beautiful shadow it was of Jesus—the ark of his people—and of the safety they find in him.

Now let us take one more look at the ark. *Let us see* HOW *it was that the blessings found in the ark were* SECURED. And in this respect, too, we shall find that it was finished and furnished: God said to Noah,—"Come thou and all thy house *into the ark.*" Gen. vii: 1. And in the

16th verse of the same chapter it is said,—"*and the Lord shut him in.*"   Noah *did* what God told him to do, and *believed* what God said to him, and in this way he was saved.   *This* was what secured to him a share of the blessings found in the ark.   Noah would not have been saved unless he had really gone into the ark as God told him to do.   It was being in the ark that saved him.   And all who were drowned by the flood were drowned *because they were not in the ark.*   Noah was not saved because he had spent a hundred and twenty years in working on the ark.   He was not saved because the ark was finished and furnished.   He was not saved because he stood without on the platform very near the door.   God said to him—"*Come into the ark.*"   He went in and stayed there and *that saved him.*

And it is just the same with us.   We cannot be saved simply because Christ has died.   We must have faith in him as our Saviour.   Jesus says,—"*Come* unto me—and I will give you rest."   Matt. xi: 28.   He says,—"*Look* unto me, and be ye saved."   Is. xlv: 22.   This means "look unto me and ye *shall be* saved."   Coming to Jesus and believing in Jesus mean expecting to be saved because of what he did and suffered for us. The best illustration of it that we can have is Noah going into the ark when God told him. Believing in Jesus is with us exactly what going into the ark was with Noah. If we do this we shall certainly be saved. If we refuse or neglect to do this we must certainly be lost; for it is written,—"There is none other name under heaven given among men, whereby we must be saved." Acts iv: 12.

This is one of the most important of all things for us to know. It is very hard to make people understand it. Let us look at one or two illustrations that may help us in trying to understand it.

The first illustration is a story told about an English nobleman. His name was Lord Congleton. He was a friend of the Earl of Shaftesbury, and a very earnest Christian man. He had a large number of people on his estate who were very poor. He tried in many ways to do them good, but found it hard to get them to believe the Bible and become Christians. This caused him great sorrow. He thought over the matter a long time. He said to himself,—"What shall I do to show these people *how* they may be saved, and secure for themselves a share in all the blessings of the gospel?" And this, you see, is the very point we are now considering. At last he hit upon a very singular plan, and at once carried it out. He made up his mind to give public notice that on a particular day, from nine o'clock in the morning to twelve o'clock at noon, he would be in his office, with his steward; and that if any of his tenants, or the people who lived on his grounds, were troubled by debts which they could not pay, if they would bring their bills with them, and tell how much they owed, they should have their debts paid, and get a receipt in full given them for the same. This notice was written out, signed by his lordship's own name, and posted up in different places. People read it, and talked about it, and wondered over it, but could not tell what to make of it.

At last the day appointed came. At nine o'clock precisely his lordship's carriage drove up to his office. He got out and entered the office, and sat there with his steward. A crowd of people gathered outside, and talked freely about this strange offer. "It's all a hoax," said one man. "I don't believe a word of it."

"But there's his lordship's own signature," replied another, "and *he* never tries to hoax people. He always means what he says."

"There must be a mistake about it some-
where," said another. "I'm not going to be
made a fool of in this way."

And thus they talked on, but no one went in.
About eleven o'clock an old man who lived
with his wife in the poor-house, came along.
He owed some money which he could not pay,
but which he greatly desired to have paid up
before he died. He had heard of this offer,
and made up his mind to accept it. Some
of his friends tried to persuade him not to go.
But he pointed to the written notice posted
against the wall. "I know," said he, "that *that's*
his lordship's name, and I'm sure he would
never put his name to anything intended to
deceive."

So he went in. "Please your lordship here's
the bill for what I owe. I am living it's true in
the poor-house; but I can't die happy while
I'm in debt."

"And why should I pay your debts?" asked
Lord Congleton. "I can't tell, please your lordship," said the old man. "But I saw the promise
signed by your lordship's own name. I had
faith in your promise, and so I came."

"Right," said his lordship. "Steward, write
him a check for his debts." The man received

it. He examined it. He saw it was all right, and then said:

"Thank your lordship a thousand times for your kindness. Now I'll go out and tell my friends."

"No, no," said Lord Congleton. "They've got the same promise that you had. If they believe my promise and come in, they shall have all that was promised. If they can't trust my word they can have nothing."

He waited in the office till the clock struck twelve. Then he went out. Waving overhead the check that had been given to him, he exclaimed, "I've got all that was promised. Three cheers for Lord Congleton. Hurrah! Hurrah! Hurrah!"

Just then his lordship came out and stepped into his carriage. Then there was a rush of men towards him, with bills in their hands crying,— "Please your lordship here's my bill—and mine —and mine." But he quietly waved his hand, and said,—"My friends, if you had believed my promise, and brought your bills in time they would all have been paid. But you would not trust me; and I can do nothing for you now."

Here is one other illustration from a laboring man:—A minister of the gospel had a man belonging to his congregation who worked in a coal mine. He was a happy Christian. In talking with him one day the minister asked him why he hoped to be saved.

"You know, sir, I'm no scholar," said the honest miner; "but I'll tell you the best way I can why I feel so happy. It's not what I do, but what Christ has done for me that I am trusting in. You've been down in the shaft of the mine. Now, for a long time I hoped to be saved, because I was trying to do what was right. But that never made me happy. I felt all the while as if I was down at the bottom of the shaft, and couldn't get out of the pit. But at last it seemed as if God said to me; 'Stop trying to lift yourself out of the shaft. When the bucket comes down just get into it, and trust to the men at the windlass to draw you out.' And so I don't try to lift myself out any more; but I trust in the Lord Jesus Christ, and leave it all to him. I used to try to do right in order that I *might* be saved. Now I know that Jesus *has* saved me, and I try to do right because I love him."

And so when we think of the *size* of the ark —of the *supplies* with which it was finished—of the *safety* found in it—and of the way in which the enjoyment of these blessings was *secured*—

we see what a beautiful shadow the ark was of the greater blessings that are offered to us in Jesus our glorious Saviour. And looking to him as the substance of this shadow, we may each of us say:

"Behold! the Ark of God!
Behold, the open door!
Hasten to gain that dear abode,
And rove my soul, no more!"

CHRIST THE BLESSING OF THE WORLD

MORE than five thousand years ago, when God gave the first promise about Christ, the expected deliverer, we were taught that he was to be a man. This is what was meant when he was spoken of in that promise as "the seed of the woman." He was to be a *human* helper, or a man. But nothing was said in that promise about the nation from which he was to come. Yet it was necessary for us to know this. If this helper was to come at all he must come from some one particular nation: and as it was important there should be no room left for doubt about him when he came, it was very necessary that it should be clearly understood beforehand from which of the many nations he was to make his appearance. And this was the next thing that God made known about Christ, the promised helper. He had already been spoken of as "the seed of the woman." This taught us that he was to be a man, that is, one of our own race. But then, nearly two thousand years after that first promise was given, God gave another promise, in which he said to Abraham,—"And in thy seed, shall all the nations of the earth be blessed." Gen. xxii: 18. And this taught us that the promised helper was not only to be a man—"the seed of the woman"—but that he was also to be—"the seed of Abraham"—or one of his descendants.

But Abraham was the head, or the founder of the Jewish nation. And so while the first promise taught us that our helper was to be a man, this second promise showed that he was to be one of the children of Abraham, or to be born of the Jewish nation. And we know that Jesus, our blessed Saviour, was a Jew. He was to be born in Bethlehem, a town belonging to the Jews. And there he *was* born. When the wise men from the east came to Jerusalem seeking him, they asked,—"Where is he that is born *King of the Jews?*" And when he hung upon the cross, the writing which Pilate placed over his head was—"*Jesus of Nazareth—the King of the Jews.*"

And the great thing which this second promise teaches is, that Jesus was to *bless the*

The Babe Lying in the Manger

And it came to pass, as the angels were gone away from them into heaven, the shepherds said one to another, Let us now go even unto Bethlehem, and see this thing which is come to pass, which the Lord hath made known unto us. And they came with haste, and found Mary, and Joseph, and the babe lying in a manger.—*St. Luke ii: 15, 16.*

NOTE BY THE ARTIST

In the households of the humbler class, the family not infrequently share the single apartment with their cattle, occupying, as in the case of the Khan before mentioned, the raised platform or "leewan," in the edge of which is the feeding trough or "manger" for the cattle. Such in all probability was the arrangement of the cave dwelling at Bethlehem which, according to tradition, provided a refuge for the Holy Family.

5

5

world.   God said to Abraham,—"In thy seed shall *all the nations of the earth be blessed.*"   In another place we are told that "all the *families* of the earth shall be blessed in him."   Gen. xii: 3. Again this blessing is promised to individual men;—Ps. lxxii: 17—and in still another place we are told that this blessing brought by Jesus was intended for "for every one of us."   Acts iii: 26.   When Jesus was on earth he said,—"I am the light of the world."   John viii: 12.   He might have said, just as truly, "I am the *blessing* of the world."   This we see was what was said of him long before he came into the world. And if it be true that Jesus was to bless all the *nations* of the world—all the *families* of the world—and all the men, or the people of the world, then we may well say that the blessing of the world was wrapped up in Jesus. When the promise of his coming was given us, it was a promise of blessing.   When he came, he came to bless.   When he began his ministry the very first thing he spoke of was the blessings he had brought to men.   There he is on the top of the mountain where he preached his first sermon.   Notice how that sermon begins.   We read,—"And seeing the multitudes, he went up into a mountain; and when he was set, his disciples came unto him: and he opened his mouth and taught them, saying, Blessed— blessed—blessed, &c." Matt. v: 1-4. He opens that sermon with a bundle of blessings. It seems as if he were so burdened with the many blessings he had brought, that he could speak of nothing else till he had spoken of them.

And as Jesus began his ministry with talking about blessings, so he continued it with scattering blessings around wherever he went. What a beautiful sketch of his life the apostle Peter gives us when he says that he "*went about doing good.*" And see what an illustration we have of this in the short sketch in Matt. iv: 23, 24. Here we are told that "Jesus went about all Galilee, teaching in their synagogues, and preaching the gospel of the kingdom, and healing all manner of diseases among the people. And they brought unto him all sick people that were taken with divers diseases and torments, and those which were possessed with devils, and those which were lunatic, and those that had the palsy, and he healed them." How well it might be said of the people whom Jesus thus healed, they were "blessed in him!" And as Jesus *began* his ministry in our world in blessing, and *continued* it in blessing, so he ended it in blessing. When his work on earth was finished, and the time had come for him to return to heaven, we read—Luke xxiv: 50, 51— how he led his disciples out to Bethany, on the top of the Mount of Olives, "and he lifted up his hands and blessed them. And it came to pass, *while he blessed them,* he was parted from them, and carried up into heaven." What a beautiful close this was to a life that was intended to be a life of blessing!

And Jesus did not cease blessing people when he went to heaven. The apostle Peter said to the Jews at Jerusalem,—"God having raised up his son Jesus sent him to *bless* you." Acts iii: 26. The mission of Jesus is to bless. As he sits at the right hand of the throne of God in heaven the great business in which he is engaged is the work of blessing men.

And if you ask how he does this, I know no better way in which to answer the question, than in the words spoken by the prophet Isaiah, when he was telling about Christ, more than seven hundred years before he was born into our world. We find these words in Isaiah lxi: 1. Our Saviour applied them to himself at the beginning of his ministry, when he was preaching at Nazareth.   He read this passage from Isaiah, in which it is written:

"The spirit of the Lord is upon me, because he has anointed me to preach the gospel to the poor; he hath sent me to heal the broken-hearted, to preach deliverance to the captives, and recovering of sight to the blind." And when he had closed the book, he said,—"This day is this scripture fulfilled in your ears." And when he had said this it was precisely as if he had said—"This prophecy refers to me. I am the person of whom Isaiah was speaking when he used these words."

Here we have clearly pointed out to us the way in which Jesus was sent to bless men. He blessed them thus, by his personal ministry while he was on earth. And since he has gone to heaven he is blessing them still, in the same way, by sending his gospel to them. And wherever people hear the gospel, and obey it, and become Christians, they find that Jesus does bless them in the way that he spoke of to the people of Nazareth. Now, if we look at these words of Jesus, we see that they refer to four ways in which he blesses people

One of these is *by giving riches to the poor.*

He says he was sent—"to preach the gospel to the poor." The word gospel means glad tidings, or good news. And what makes this gospel good news is, that it tells us of the grace of God that Jesus brings. This grace is what we all need more than anything else. If we really get this grace it will make us rich. It will be worth more to us than all the wealth in the world. It will do for us what no earthly treasure could do. It will secure to us the pardon of our sins. It will change our evil hearts and make them good. It will help us to love and serve God. It will open the door of heaven to us, and make us fit to go in, and live there in happiness for ever.

And this is the way in which Jesus himself speaks of the grace of God; for this is what he means, when he says,—"I counsel thee to buy of me *gold tried in the fire, that thou mayest be rich.*" Rev. iii: 18. Those who have this grace are rich indeed. They are "rich towards God." They have a treasure laid up in heaven, "where moth and rust do not corrupt, nor thieves break through and steal." That is a treasure that none can take from us, and it will last forever. And when Jesus was preaching the gospel to the poor; when he was telling them about the grace of God, and urging them to seek it, it might well be said that he was giving riches to the poor.   And when he sends out his ministers to preach, and his servants to teach the blessed gospel, he is still doing the same thing.   This gospel tell us of the grace of God, and teaches us how to get it.   However much of the riches of this world we may have, our souls must be poor if we have not the grace of God in them. And however little of this world's wealth we have, our souls are rich if only the grace of God is ours.   We may well look up to Jesus and say, as a good man once said:

> " Give what thou wilt, *without Thee* we are poor,
> But, *with Thee rich*, take what thou wilt away ! "

"A Poor Rich Minister."—I saw an account lately of a good Methodist minister who was so well satisfied with the hope of these heavenly riches that he was not willing to own any of the riches of this world.   He was very poor, and his family were sometimes in want of things necessary to their comfort.   A rich farmer belonging to his congregation, and who loved him greatly, made him a present of a farm containing a number of acres, and gave him the title-deed to the property.   The minister thanked his kind friend for his generous gift, and went home feeling very happy. But, about three months after this, he called one day on his good friend the farmer. After talking together for awhile the minister handed to his friend a roll of parchment saying: "Here, sir, I want to give you back the title-deed to your farm."

"Why, what's the matter?" asked the astonished farmer. "Is there anything wrong about it?"

"No, sir."

"Well, isn't the land good?"

"There's none better in the State."

"Do you think I grudge having given it to you?"

"Not at all; I know how truly generous you are."

"Then why don't you keep it?"

"Well, sir," said the minister, "you know I am very fond of singing. And there is one hymn in our book the singing of which has been the greatest comfort of my life. But I haven't been able to sing it with my whole heart since I owned this farm. This hymn says:

"No foot of land do I possess,
No cottage in the wilderness,
A poor wayfaring man.

" I lodge awhile in tents below,
Or gladly wander to and fro,
Till I my Canaan gain.

" *There* is my house and portion fair,
My treasure and my heart are there,
And my abiding home."

"I am very grateful, my good friend, for your kindness," said the minister, "but please take back your title-deed; for I would rather be able to sing that hymn, with all my heart, as I have been used to sing it, than own all the farms in this State."

Now, I cannot but think that this good minister was a little too particular. But one thing is very clear, *he did feel that the gospel of Jesus had made him rich.* He had a treasure in heaven, and the hope of it made him contented and happy, even though he had none of the riches of this world. The blessing of the world is in Jesus, and one of the ways in which he blesses men is by *giving riches to the poor.*

But another way in which Jesus blesses men is—BY GIVING COMFORT TO THE SORROWING.

This is what he taught when he said that he was sent to—"*heal the broken-hearted.*" If you break a bowl, or a pitcher that is full of water, of course, all the water in it will run out. Now, the heart in the midst of our body is sometimes compared to a bowl or pitcher. Eccles. xii: 6. And if the point of a sword, or a bullet from a gun or pistol penetrates a man's heart he must die, because his heart is literally broken or pierced. But sometimes we speak of persons being broken-hearted, not in a literal, but a figurative sense. We only mean by it that they are in great sorrow. And in this sense to heal those who are broken-hearted, means to give them comfort in their sorrow. And so, when Jesus said that he was sent to heal the broken-hearted, he meant he was to give comfort to the sorrowing. And when we come to read in the New Testament the life of Jesus, we see how he was doing this all the time.

The widow of Nain was a sorrowing, broken-hearted woman, as she was following the dead body of her only son to the grave. But, when Jesus raised that dead young man to life again, and gave him back to his mother, we know that he was healing the broken-hearted, or giving comfort to the sorrowing.

And so it was when he raised Lazarus from the grave, and sent him back alive, and well, to his broken-hearted sisters at Bethany. And as Jesus went up and down the land of Israel, healing the sick, cleansing the lepers, making the lame to walk, the deaf to hear, the dumb to speak, and the blind to see, we can understand how truly it might be said of him that he was healing the broken-hearted, or giving comfort to the sorrowing.

And this is what Jesus has been doing ever since. This is what he is still doing to bless the world, wherever the Bible makes him known. Let us look at one or two illustrations of the way in which Jesus blesses men.

"The Happy Deaf Mute."—During an examination in an institution for the Deaf and Dumb one of the examiners wrote on the blackboard, this question: "Who made the world?" One of the scholars, a boy about twelve or fourteen years old, took the chalk and wrote this answer:—"In the beginning *God* created the heavens and the earth." The next question was: "Why did Jesus Christ come into the world?" A smile of grateful love lighted up the boy's face as he wrote: "This is a faithful saying, and worthy of all acceptation that Christ Jesus came into the world to save sinners." Then the gentleman wrote this question: "How is it that *you* were born deaf and dumb, while I can both speak and hear?" This was a hard question to put to that poor boy; but without a moment's hesitation he took up the chalk again, and with a look of quiet peace and resignation on his face, he wrote these words: "Even so, Father, for so it seemed good in thy sight!" Ah! that dear boy had been with Jesus. He had blessed him by giving him comfort in his sorrow.

"Blue Sky Inside."—"It's too bad to see how hard it rains," said Bessie Jones, looking out of the window, with an angry scowl upon her face. "It's very provoking. It always rains when I don't want it to. It's spoiling the slides, and there wont be an inch of ice left in an hour to skate on. Now where's my fun this afternoon, I should like to know?"

"Well, you can stay at home, and sew," said her aunt.

"But I don't want to sew," was Bessie's cross reply; "I want to skate. I declare this rain is *too* provoking."

"The provoking is all in your own heart, Bessie," said her brother Charley, who was a little older than Bessie, and was trying to be a Christian. "If you only had blue sky inside," he went on to say, "you wouldn't mind much about the rain outside."

Hurrah! for Bessie's brother Charley! *"Blue sky inside!"* That is a beautiful thought. We have no power to prevent the rain and the storms from coming. But if we can only find out how to make "blue sky inside," the rain and the storms will not trouble us much. And this is just what Jesus came to help us do. This is one of the ways in which he blesses the world. And if we would all learn from him how to make "blue sky inside," what a happy world this would be! Then the promise given to Abraham would be fulfilled, when God said to him—"In thy seed shall all the families of the earth be blessed."

"The Solitary Feast."—In a certain alms-house there was an old colored woman. She had no relative in the world, and no money but what visitors sometimes gave her. But she was a true Christian. She had known many sorrows, but Jesus had blessed her by giving her comfort and strength to bear them. They called her "Aunty." She was too feeble to leave her room, and so she used to hold service by herself on Sundays; and once a month she was in the habit of taking the communion all alone. A Christian lady, who sometimes visited that alms-house, went there one Sunday morning. She generally visited "Aunty" in her room. On hearing that this was the day on which she took the communion by herself, she asked the matron to let her stand outside the open door, that she might see the good old Christian go through this service, without knowing that any one was near. And this is the account given by that lady of what she saw and heard:

"What I saw was a picture for a painter. The door, which was opposite a raised window, was partly open. A vine had climbed up the wire grating of the window, and was filled with blossoms. The fragrance came in on the Sabbath air with the bright sunshine.

"There on a bench sat the old woman, not knowing that any one was near. Her dress was clean and neatly ironed, and the cap upon her head was as white as snow. Before her was a little pine table, covered with a clean white cotton cloth. There was nothing on the table but a white earthen plate, on which were a few small pieces of bread, and an earthen teacup filled with water, while at her side lay a Bible and a small hymn-book.

"She began the service by singing from memory two or three verses of an old communion hymn. Then she opened the Bible and read the story of the crucifixion as given by St. Matthew.

"At the close of her reading she reverently repeated the words: 'The Lord Jesus, the same night he was betrayed took bread and blessed it;'—then holding the plate of bread in her hands upon the table, she bowed her head in silent prayer. Then she went on with the Bible words,—'Take, eat; this is my body, given for you. Do this in remembrance of me.' As she spoke these words, she took a piece of bread from the plate, and with closed eyes, in silence and in tears she ate the bread. Again she sang a verse,—'Nearer my God, to thee, &c.' Then she went on with the Bible words,—'After the same manner also he took the cup, and gave thanks;' and with the tea-cup of water in her hand, she again offered prayer; but this time, though her voice was low, almost a whisper, I was able to catch her words. As I listened I lost sight of the almshouse, and felt almost as if I were in heaven.

"When her prayer and thanksgiving were over, she solemnly took the cup, and, as she lifted it to her lips, repeated the words of Jesus,—'Drink ye all of this; this cup is the New Testament in my blood, for the remission of sins; do this

The Child Jesus Brought to the Temple

And when the days of her purification according to the law of Moses were accomplished, they brought him to Jerusalem, to present *him* to the Lord. And to offer a sacrifice according to that which is said in the law of the Lord, A pair of turtledoves, or two young pigeons. And, behold, there was a man in Jerusalem, whose name *was* Simeon; and the same man *was* just and devout, waiting for the consolation of Israel: and the Holy Ghost was upon him. And it was revealed unto him by the Holy Ghost, that he should not see death, before he had seen the Lord's Christ. And he came by the Spirit into the temple: and when the parents brought in the child Jesus, to do for him after the custom of the law. Then took he him up in his arms, and blessed God, and said, Lord, now lettest thou thy servant depart in peace.—*St. Luke ii: 22, 24–29.*

NOTE BY THE ARTIST

The scene is laid at the foot of the fifteen steps which, in Herod's temple, led from the second court (the Court of the Women) through the Nicanor Gate to the Inner, or court of the priests, in which stood the altar of sacrifice in front of the Temple proper.

6

in remembrance of me.' Then she drank from the cup, and setting it down on the table, again bowed her head in silent prayer. Then suddenly raising her head she exclaimed,— 'Hallelujah! Glory to God!'—a sweet smile like that of an angel lighting up her dark face —'I sees de gates,' she said, looking up to the ceiling of the room—'I sees de door ob heben open! I hear de angels singing! Yes, I's on de road! I's almost home! Hallelujah!' Then she sang:

> " ' I'm but a traveller here,
> Heaven is my home.'

"At the close of the service she turned, and saw me standing at the door. 'Why, chile,' she said, 'I didn't know you was here. I thought there was no one near old "Aunty" but de blessed Lord, and de angels.'"

Now Jesus had been with that poor old colored woman and blessed her. He had healed her broken heart, and given her comfort in her sorrow. She was alone in the almshouse, but even there Jesus had made her happy, and taught her how to make "blue sky inside." And if he can make an almshouse seem like heaven, then we see how able he is to bless men anywhere and everywhere.

Vol. I—6

Another way in which Jesus blesses men is by GIVING LIBERTY TO THE CAPTIVES.

It is a sad sight to see men bound with chains, so that they cannot use their limbs. And if they are shut up in prison, as well as bound with chains this is still more sad. But there are chains and prisons for the souls of men, as well as for their bodies. If we give way to any sin, that sin binds our souls so that they can have no more freedom of action than our bodies would have if they were bound in chains of iron.

This is what is meant in one of the beautiful collects of our church, in which we pray that we may "be delivered from the bands of those sins which by our frailty we have committed." And this is the reason why the Bible speaks of men as being—*"taken captive by Satan* at his will." II. Tim. ii: xxvi. He tempts men to commit sins, and then binds them in the chains of those sins; and in this way they are made his prisoners or captives. And when Jesus seeks a poor sinner, and converts him by his grace; when he delivers him from the power of his sins, changes his heart, and helps him to lead a new life, then it is that he is blessing that man by giving liberty to the captive.

But there are no chains that Satan makes for men so strong as those which he fastens on the soul of the poor drunkard. He is bound hand and foot. The prison in which he is made captive has walls so thick, and doors so strongly bolted and barred, that he never can get out by any effort of his own. But Jesus is able to break the strongest chain by which any poor drunkard was ever bound, and to open the prison door in spite of all the bolts and bars that may secure it.

Here is an illustration of this statement which I know to be true:

One day, while Mr. Moody was preaching in our city, I received a letter written by a person who signed himself "A Reformed Drunkard." He wished me to read his letter in the noonday meeting for the encouragement of those who were trying to break loose from the chains by which the drunkard is bound. And I did read it there. The writer of this letter called to see me before I read it in public, that I might be sure it was all right. I was surprised at his appearance, when I saw him. He was as fine-looking, gentlemanly a man as I had ever seen. He was intelligent and well educated. This was his story, as briefly as I can give it:

"My family," he said, "is one of the most respectable in Philadelphia. They belong to the Society of Friends. My mother, now in heaven, was formerly a preacher in the Society. For seven years I had been a confirmed drunkard. By this terrible evil I had lost my money, my business, my character, my health, my friends, and my self-respect. It had even separated me from my wife and family, and made me an outcast from society. I was lost to all that was good. I had tried again and again to stop drinking, but in vain. I had taken different medicines, and had signed the temperance pledge a number of times, but without any benefit. Everybody said my case was hopeless. At last when I was in a public hospital, sick, with that dreadful disease, which drunkenness causes, called 'delirium tremens,' and was given up to die, *then*, as I believe, in answer to the prayers of my sainted mother, I was led to look to Jesus. I called on him for help. He heard my cry, and helped me. By the power of his grace he broke the strong chains of that dreadful sin by which I had been bound, and which nothing but the grace of God can break. I rose from my sick bed a changed man. By the help which Jesus gave me I was able to stop drinking.

And now, for months, I have been a sober man. I am restored to health, to happiness, and usefulness; to my friends and to my family, and am on the way to heaven, where I hope to meet that beloved mother through whose prayers I have been saved."

Such was this man's story. Here we see how Jesus gives deliverance to the captives. And what he did for this poor prisoner of sin and Satan, he is able and willing to do for all who call upon him. And if he has power to help men in this way, then it may well be said that he was "sent to bless them."

But there is another way in which Jesus was sent to bless men, and that is by giving—SIGHT TO THE BLIND. When he was on earth, he met those who had been blind for years, and others who were born blind, and he opened their eyes.

We find blind people everywhere. Every city and town and village has some blind people in it. Happily the blind are few, compared to those who see. This is true when we speak about the blindness of the bodily eye. But it is very different when we speak about the blindness of the soul. We are all born blind in this sense. None of us ever see with the eyes of our souls till Jesus comes and opens them.

We do not see what sinners we are: we do not see what a terrible evil sin is: we do not see the fearful danger we are in of being lost forever, and we do not see that Jesus is the only one who can save us from this great danger. But when Jesus comes and opens the eyes of our souls, then it is as if we had been brought into a new world. We see what great sinners we have been, and we feel sad and sorry for it. We see what a precious Saviour Jesus is, and we begin to love him. We see what a blessed home he is preparing for us in yonder glorious heaven, and we make up our minds that by God's help we will try and be with him there. This is just what Jesus was doing when he was on earth. This is what Jesus is doing now, and in this way he is doing good all the time, wherever the Bible is known. Here is an illustration of the way in which Jesus opens the eyes of those people whose souls are blind.

Some time ago a Christian lady was looking out of her parlor window in the city of London, when she saw a poor blind beggar in front of her house. He had a violin in a bag hanging from his neck. In his right hand he had a cane or staff to lean on, while his left hand held a string that was fastened to the collar on the neck of his dog—his only guide, as he groped his way in darkness through the crowded streets of that busy city. The poor man looked cold, hungry, and sad. The lady pitied him, and sent her servant to ask him to come into the house, to get warmed, and rested, and have something to eat. The servant led the blind man and his dog up the steps into the dining room, and gave him a nice warm place by the fireside. As he sat there, with his dog lying beside him, the blind beggar showed his thankfulness by the smile that brightened his face, while the poor dog tried to say, "Thank you! thank you!" as well as he could by wagging his tail.

While he was eating his dinner, the good lady sat by and talked with the poor man.

"How long have you been blind, my friend?"

"Fifteen years, ma'am. I had an attack of small-pox, and it took away my eyesight."

"And have you been begging all that time?"

"No, ma'am; only a few years. I had two brothers who kindly took care of me; but they both died three years ago, and now I have no one to do anything for me; so I have to go out and beg."

"Can you play any hymns, or psalms, or sacred pieces?"

"No, ma'am; I only know two pieces, and they are both songs, or ballads. An old sailor taught me both of them."

"But there are many beautiful hymns, and sweet psalm-tunes that would sound well in the streets. People would like to hear them, and you would get more pennies in your little basket for singing them."

"I do not know any hymns, ma'am; I wish I did."

"Well, while you are getting your dinner, I will repeat one of my favorite hymns to you, and then I'll sing it; and when you have done, you must see if you can play it and sing it: will you?"

"Yes, ma'am, I will, and thank you for it."

Then the lady recited one of Dr. Watt's hymns:

> "Not all the blood of beasts,
>   On Jewish altars slain,
> Could give the guilty conscience peace,
>   Or wash away its stain.
>
> "But Christ the heavenly Lamb,
>   Takes all our sins away;
> A sacrifice of nobler name
>   And richer blood than they.

"My faith would lay her hand
    On that dear head of thine,
While like a penitent I stand,
    And there confess my sin.

"My soul looks back to see
    The burden thou didst bear,
When hanging on the cursed tree,
    And hopes her guilt was there.

"Believing, we rejoice
    To see the curse removed;
We bless the lamb with cheerful voice,
    And sing his bleeding love."

She repeated this hymn slowly and deliberately two or three times. Then she sang it to a very sweet tune. She had a fine, full voice. The blind man stopped eating to listen. With his face upraised to the ceiling, he rolled his sightless eyeballs in evident delight. Even the dog seemed to forget his crumbs and his bones, and wagged his tail vigorously.

"Would you please sing it for me again, ma'am," said the blind man.

She sang it again and again. He seemed to take in every word of the hymn, and every note of the music. When he had finished his dinner, he took his violin, and standing in the middle of the room, he struck up the tune the lady had been singing, and went through the whole hymn. The lady was delighted, and so was the poor blind fiddler. Then he repeated it, so as to be sure he had it right, and thanking the lady for her kindness, he went on his way.

About two months after this, the blind beggar, with his dog, called again at that lady's house. She shook hands with him and said:

"Well, my friend, I'm glad to see you; how does the new music answer?"

"Wonderfully well, ma'am. I've just called to tell you about it; but I don't know how. The day I called here—oh! that blessed day!— and several days after, I sang pretty well; but one day I couldn't sing at all."

"Why? had you taken cold?"

"No, ma'am; but I had a guilty conscience. It was, as that hymn says, all stained with sin. The oftener I sang those lines, the worse I felt. The verses described my case exactly. I was a penitent. I remained in the house all day in great sorrow. My dog knows when I'm in trouble, and he would come and put his paws on my knee, saying, as plainly as he could, 'What's the matter, master?'

"I thought about the verses, though I could not play them nor sing them; but the last

verse led me to trust in Jesus, and now, indeed,
I can

"'Bless the Lamb with cheerful voice,
And sing his bleeding love.'

"Before that, my soul was blind as well as my
body; but now I have new eyes. Jesus has
opened the eyes of my soul. I see him as my
Saviour, my Lord and my God. I thank you for
calling me in that day, and teaching me that
precious hymn. Oh! ma'am, that was a blessed
day to me. I was blind then, both in soul and
in body; but Jesus has given eyesight to my
soul, and now I see with *new eyes*."

And this shows us how Jesus blesses men by
giving sight to the blind; and when we put
these four things together, and remember how
Jesus is engaged continually in giving *riches to
the poor*, and *comfort to the sorrowing*, and *liberty
to the captives*, and *eyesight to the blind*, wherever
the sound of the gospel is heard, we see how
true the promise is which God gave to Abraham
when he said: "And in thy seed shall all the
families of the earth be blessed." And when,
at last, this precious gospel is "truly preached,
truly received, and truly followed" in every land,
then indeed it will be true, that *all the world
will be blessed in Jesus*."

But there is one difficulty in this subject that should be looked at before leaving it. Some one may ask this question: Are there not multitudes of people in Africa and in Asia and in the islands of the sea who have never heard of Jesus, and have never received any of the spiritual blessings of which we have been speaking? Certainly there are. Then how can it be said that "*all* the families of the earth" have been blessed in him? This is a fair, honest question. Let us see if we cannot give a fair, honest answer to it.

Now, we must remember that all the blessings of which we have been speaking, as those which Jesus gives to men, are spiritual blessings. They belong to the soul and to the life that is to come. But there is another class of blessings that we owe to Jesus. These belong to the body and to the life we have in this present world. But this life itself, with health and strength and food and clothing and all our present comforts, is embraced in this class of blessings. *We owe all these to Jesus.* They were all forfeited by sin, and bought back to us by the death of Christ.

Before the missionaries of the gospel went to the islands of the South Sea, there was a heathen custom there called *taboo*, which well illustrates this part of our subject. The heathen priests in those islands, when they wanted anything for their idols, used to say that it was tabooed —that is, it belonged to their gods—and then no one dared touch it. A tabooed thing was a forfeited thing. But when Adam and Eve sinned, they forfeited life, and breath, and air, and water and food. All these things were tabooed; we had lost our right to them. But when Jesus agreed to bear the punishment due to our sins, he took off the taboo; he recovered for us all that we had forfeited. And now every ray of light that brightens this world, every drop of water, and every particle of food that we enjoy, the air we breathe, the clothes we wear, our friends, our homes, and all that helps to make us comfortable and happy in this life, we owe to Jesus; and those who never heard of Jesus are indebted to him for these blessings, although they do not know it. And so we see how true it is, according to the promise made to Abraham, that "*in his seed all* the families of the earth are blessed." In this sense they *have all* been blessed from the beginning. They are blessed every day.

The blessing of the world is in Jesus.

The Three Wise Men

Now when Jesus was born in Bethlehem of Judea in the days of Herod the king, behold, there came wise men from the east to Jerusalem, Saying, Where is he that is born King of the Jews? for we have seen his star in the east, and are come to worship him. When Herod the king had heard *these things*, he was troubled, and all Jerusalem with him. And when he had gathered all the chief priests and scribes of the people together, he demanded of them where Christ should be born. And they said unto him, In Bethlehem of Judea: for thus it is written by the prophet. Then Herod, when he had privily called the wise men, enquired of them diligently what time the star appeared. And he sent them to Bethlehem, and said, Go and search diligently for the young child; and when ye have found *him*, bring me word again, that I may come and worship him also.—*St. Matt. ii: 1–5, 7, 8.*

NOTE BY THE ARTIST

The space immediately within the city gate is frequently used as a market place, and that at Jerusalem during the period of Roman occupation would certainly be the post of a military guard. The three wise men representing the cultures of Persia, India, and China, are in harmony with that insatiable thirst for knowledge which made such men travel.

7

JOSEPH AND JESUS COMPARED

WHENEVER we hear or read about Joseph, we think of Egypt; and what a wonderful country Egypt is! It is the country of that grand old river Nile. There, too, are the famous Pyramids. People go from the ends of the earth to visit them. They climb their steep sides; they stand on the top of them, and look out over all the country around; then they go down into that dark chamber, which is in the centre of the largest Pyramid. Near the Pyramids is the celebrated Sphinx. This is a strange-looking figure, with the head of a woman and the body of a lion, cut out of the solid rock on which the great Pyramid stands. The greater part of it is now covered up with sand; but some years ago, when the sand was removed, the body of the huge figure was found to measure a hundred and forty-three feet in length, and from its feet to the top of its head

it was between sixty and seventy feet high.
What a wonderful country Egypt appears to
have been to make such great works as these!
Now, this was the country in which Joseph
spent the greater part of his life.

The history of Joseph is one of the most
interesting in the Old Testament. We love to
hear about it when we are young; and even
when we grow up to be men and women we
never get tired of hearing or reading the history
of Joseph; and one reason why we love this
sweet story so much is not only because such
strange things happened to Joseph, but because
there is so much in his life that reminds us of
Jesus and seems to point to him.

If you look at the first line in the last book
of the Bible, you will find that it reads thus:
"The Revelation of Jesus Christ." This shows
us what that book was written for: it was to
reveal, or to make known to us, things about
Jesus, great things and wonderful things, which
it was important for us to know, but which we
never could have known if God had not been
pleased to tell us of them; and so we call that
last book in the Bible, the book of the Revelation, or, as we generally express it, "the book of
Revelations." There are many revelations in it

about Jesus; and this is true of the Old Testament as well as the New. It is true of the *first* book in the Bible as well as of the *last*. Every part of the Bible was intended by God to teach us something about his blessed Son, and so to be a revelation of Jesus Christ; and this is what the apostle John teaches us when he says,— "The testimony of Jesus is the spirit of prophecy." Rev. xix: 10. This means that all the prophets, or Old Testament writers, had something to tell of Jesus. *This* was the most important thing they had to do; and when our Saviour was on earth he taught his disciples that "the law of Moses, the Psalms and the prophets" had many things in them about him which would all come to pass. Luke xxiv: 44. And so the book of Genesis has in it many things intended to teach us about Jesus. *The story of Joseph is full of Jesus.* I wish now to speak of Joseph and Jesus compared. There are *five* things in Joseph's history which give us beautiful illustrations of the character and work of Jesus.

In the first place, Joseph was sent on A MISSION *by his father.*

At the time when this took place, Jacob, the father of Joseph, was living in the vale of Hebron. The city of Hebron is still in existence,

and it is one of the oldest cities in the world.
Abraham and Isaac lived there for the greater
part of their lives, and there they were buried
in the cave of Machpelah. There Jacob himself
was buried. He died in Egypt, but, before his
death, he made Joseph solemnly promise to
carry him up to the land of Canaan, and bury
him in the same grave with his father Isaac, and
his grandfather Abraham; and Joseph did so.
Gen. xlvii: 29-31; l: 1-14.

When the Israelites came into the land of
Canaan, Hebron was made one of the cities of
refuge. Joshua xx: 1-7. David was made king
in Hebron, and here he reigned over Judah for
seven years. The city of Hebron was situated
in a valley; and when Joseph was sent forth by
his father, we are told that "he sent him forth
out of the vale of Hebron." Gen. xxxvii: 14.
This was a very fertile valley. Vines and fig-
trees and pomegranates flourished here, and it
was here that the famous grapes known as "the
grapes of Eshcol" grew. When the spies whom
Moses sent to search the land of Canaan came
back, among the fruits they brought as speci-
mens was a bunch of these grapes. It was so
large that they had to put it on a pole which
was borne by two men upon their shoulders.

There were two pools in this valley, and here also grew the famous old tree known as "Abraham's Oak." How fertile and beautiful "the vale of Hebron" must have looked when Joseph went out from it, at his father's bidding to seek his brethren! How little Joseph knew, when he went out that morning, that he was never to come back again! He thought he was only going to be absent for a few days. But *that* was the last time he was ever to look on that fine old town, and the beautiful vale around it, with its pools of water, its fertile vines, and its famous trees. When we leave home in the morning we never know what may happen before night. And Joseph was made to feel this deeply.

Joseph's brethren were shepherds. They had large flocks of sheep. They had taken these flocks to a place called Shechem. It is now called Nablus, and lies at the foot of Mount Gerizim, in a valley between that mountain and Mount Ebal. The land in this part of the country is very fertile. There is plenty of grass and water there, so that it afforded good pasture for sheep and cattle. This was the place to which Joseph was sent by his father. It was about sixty miles distant from Hebron. Joseph had to go on foot, alone, and among strangers. So it was quite a serious undertaking for a lad of seventeen years of age. And here we see how Joseph *was sent on a mission.*

And this is the first thing about Joseph in which he reminds us of Jesus. And it is a beautiful illustration of what Jesus did. He came from heaven on a mission from his father. He was *"the sent one."* He was the first missionary. When he was on earth he spoke of himself as the one "whom the father had sanctified and *sent into the world."*

When Jacob called Joseph to send him on this mission he answered at once, "here am I." He listened to his father's instructions, and went without a moment's delay. And when Jesus knew that God, his father, wished to send him into this world he was ready at once to do his father's will. He said,—"Lo! I come to do thy will. I delight to do it. Yea, thy law is within my heart." Ps. xl: 7, 8. And thus, when we think how Joseph was sent on a mission by his father, and how willing he was to go, he reminds us of Jesus, in this respect: they were both sent on a mission.

But there is one thing in this part of our subject in which Joseph was very different from

Jesus.   When Joseph was sent out by his father from the vale of Hebron, he had no knowledge at all of what was before him.   He had not the least idea of what he was to suffer.   He knew nothing of the pit into which his brethren were to cast him; nor the slavery into which they would sell him; nor the gloomy prison in Egypt, where he was to be a prisoner for years.   If Jacob had known anything about this, he never would have sent his darling Joseph on that mission.   And if Joseph had known of it, he would, no doubt, have been unwilling to go. But Jesus—our Joseph—knew what was before him when he came on his merciful mission. He saw it all before he came.   He knew about the manger in Bethlehem; the temptation in the wilderness; the poverty, and toil, and weariness; the persecution; "the agony and bloody sweat;" —the mocking, the scourging, the crowning with thorns, the crucifixion, the death, and the burial.   All this was perfectly well known to him; and yet he came.   How wonderful this was!   This is the first point in the comparison. Joseph was sent on a mission by his father, and so was Jesus.

But Joseph was sent on this mission to show his father's LOVE *for his children: and so it was with*

Jesus. This is the second point of the comparison.

When Joseph went out of the vale of Hebron to seek his brethren, it was not for his own benefit that he went, or that of his father; for Jacob was a rich man. He had everything necessary for his comfort and that of his family. He was not seeking his own wealth or honor, or pleasure when he sent forth his darling Joseph on that long and dangerous journey. He was doing it for the good of his other sons. They had wandered far away from home with their flocks. He had not heard from them for a long time. They might be in want or in danger. The thought of them was a care to him. He longed to hear how they were getting on. And he wished them to know that although they had done wrong, their father still thought of them; and would gladly welcome them to their old home again. And how many a poor wanderer has been saved from ruin by just such a kind message from a loving father! Here is an illustration:

"The Wanderer Restored."—Some time ago, a gentleman in Boston named Johnson, had a son who went to California. There he fell into bad company and became intemperate. His father wrote for him to come home; but he would not come. Years passed on, and the hearts of his parents were grieved greatly to hear from time to time of his wrong doings. One Spring a friend of Mr. Johnson was going to California on business. When bidding him good-by, Mr. Johnson said to him, "If you should happen to meet my poor George, tell him I love him still, and shall be glad to have him come home again."

On arriving in California this gentleman inquired for George Johnson; but no one seemed to know anything about him. At last he learned where he was. One night he followed him to the wretched saloon, where he spent most of his time in drinking and gambling. He saw him put down the last dollar he had on the gambling table. He lost it. Almost crazy with drink and shame, he was about to rush out of the room, and end his miserable life by blowing out his brains. Just then "His own friend, and his father's friend," laid his hand gently on his shoulder, and spoke in tones of kindness to him of his better days, of his home, and his friends there. "And, George," he added, "the last thing your father said to me, on parting was, 'if you see my poor boy, tell him I love him still, and would gladly welcome him back to his old home.'" Those loving words had a strange effect on George. He became calm and quiet. He bowed his head and wept. Then like the prodigal he said,—"I will arise and go to my father." He did so. He met a warm and loving welcome. His whole course of life was changed, and he became a useful, happy man. The thing that saved him was that loving message from his father.

And when we think of the purpose for which Joseph was sent to his brethren, what a beautiful illustration we have of the purpose for which Jesus—our Joseph—came into this world!

When our Father in heaven sent Jesus on his mission to us, it was not because he needed us, or anything that belonged to us. He was *very* rich. He had enough in himself, and in heaven, to make him perfectly happy, even if we, and our world had been destroyed. But he knew how different it was with us. He knew that we had sinned. We had gone away from him, like the prodigal son, and had gotten into trouble. He knew also that we never could get back to him, or ever be happy again, without his help. And he wanted us to know that he remembered us, and loved us still, and that he wished us to come back to him. This is what he sent Jesus into our world for. And this is what Jesus tells us in that beautiful passage—John iii: 16—when he says: *"God so loved the world that he gave his only begotten Son, that whosoever believeth in him should not perish, but have everlasting life."*

This is the most wonderful verse in the Bible. If I were told that the Bible was to be destroyed, and that I could only have one verse out of it, to keep in memory, as long as I lived, I think I should prefer this verse to any other. It seems as if the whole Bible had been pressed into this single verse. It teaches the precious truth that God loves us, and that Jesus was sent into the world as a proof of God's love. If any one should ask me, What is the sweetest view of God's character that the Bible gives? I would point to that little verse with only these words in it,—*God is love.* I. John iv: 8. And then, if I were asked for the proof or illustration of God's love, I would point to Bethlehem with its manger, and Calvary with its cross. The object of Joseph's mission to his brethren was to show his father's love to them. And Jesus was like Joseph in this respect. The object of Christ's mission into our world was to show God's love to us.

But, in the third place, Joseph's mission to his brethren brought him into GREAT TROUBLE. *And here we have another illustration of Jesus and his work.*

Joseph's trouble began as soon as he came to his brethren. He had sought them first in Shechem, but could not find them there. We read that "A certain man found him wandering in the field; and the man asked him, saying, What seekest thou? And he said, I seek my brethren: tell me I pray thee where they feed their flocks. And the man said, They are departed hence; for I heard them say, Let us go to Dothan. And Joseph went after his brethren and found them in Dothan." Gen. xxxvii: 15-17. Dothan was about twenty miles north of Shechem. I remember looking at it with great interest, as we passed by it on our way from Samaria to Nazareth. And as I saw shepherds with their flocks there still, I thought of Joseph and his brethren. The sons of Jacob had done with their flocks just what the shepherds in that country do to-day. When the pasture failed in one part of the country, they removed to other places, wherever they could find good pasture.

Joseph came to his brethren at Dothan with his heart full of love. He thought, no doubt,

how glad they would be to see him, and how
happy he would be to tell them of their dear
old father, and all the news about home.   But,
poor fellow! what a disappointment awaited
him! How differently his brethren felt towards
him! When they saw him coming towards
them, they said,—"Behold, this *dreamer* cometh!
Come now, therefore, and let us slay him, and
cast him into a pit; and we will say, some evil
beast hath devoured him; and we shall see what
will become of his dreams." Gen. xxxvii: 19, 20.
And when he came up they would not listen to
anything he had to say about their home, or
their father.   But they rudely tore off his coat
of many colors, and cast him into a pit.   Poor
Joseph, this was the beginning of his trouble!
Then they sold him to the Midianites, to carry
him down to Egypt as a slave. We can imagine
how earnestly Joseph would plead with his
brethren, for their father's sake not to do this.
But they would not listen. They were reminded
of this many years after, and it caused them
great sorrow. See Gen. xlii: 21.   Thus Joseph
was torn from the happy home where he had
lived, like the son of a prince, and carried down
to Egypt as a slave. The road over which he
travelled in going to Egypt, brought him at one

place near to Hebron. We can imagine Joseph's great sorrow when he reached that part of the road. "Yonder, is Hebron," he would say to himself, "where my happy home is: and where my dear old father lives! O, if he only knew what happened to me! But now I shall never see my home and my father again!" This was part of Joseph's trouble.

And now he is in Egypt—a stranger among strangers. The language, the customs, the religion of the people are all so different from what he has been accustomed to at home! We are not told how Joseph felt at this time; but we know well how we should feel under such circumstances, and we may be sure that Joseph felt just as we should do.

We know how Joseph prospered at first in Egypt. Then, after awhile, we know how that wicked woman, the wife of his master, told falsehoods about him, and caused him to lose his office, and to be cast into prison, like a thief or a murderer. This must have been the darkest hour in Joseph's life. No doubt Satan came to him, while in prison and tempted him to think that there was no God, or else he would not be allowed to suffer so much, simply because he would not consent to do what he knew to be

Adoration of the Wise Men

When they had heard the king, they departed; and, lo, the star, which they saw in the east, went before them, till it came and stood over where the young child was. When they saw the star, they rejoiced with exceeding great joy. And when they were come into the house, they saw the young child with Mary his mother, and fell down, and worshipped him: and when they had opened their treasures, they presented unto him gifts; gold, and frankincense, and myrrh. And being warned of God in a dream that they should not return to Herod, they departed into their own country another way.—*St. Matt. ii: 9–12.*

NOTE BY THE ARTIST

Mediæval tradition based in the first instance upon a liberal acceptance of Is. lx: 1–3 is responsible for the otherwise unsupported supposition that the "Wise Men" of the gospel were kings. It would seem equally justifiable to believe that these may have been holy and humble men of heart, searching toward the Higher Light through the twilight afforded by the three great Eastern religions which bear the names of Brahma, Zoroaster, and Buddha.

8

8

wrong. But we know that Joseph did not listen to these thoughts. He held fast to his trust in God. For even in that Egyptian prison, we are told that "The Lord was with Joseph, and gave him favor with the keeper of the prison; and that which he did the Lord made to prosper." Gen. xxxix: 21-23. And when we think of the trouble that came to Joseph from the mission on which his father sent him, we see how much there is in this part of Joseph's life to remind us of Jesus.

When Joseph came to his brethren to tell them about their home and their father they would not listen to him. And when Jesus came to the Jews, who were his brethren by birth, to tell them about the great love of their Father they would not hear him. We read, in John i: 11: "he came to his own and his own received him not." The sinful treatment which Joseph received from his brethren caused him to shed bitter tears. And when Jesus was in the garden of Gethsemane, the sins of his brethren, brought such an agony upon him that "his sweat was, as it were, great drops of blood falling down to the ground." Luke xxii: 44. And in that agony the apostle Paul tells us "he offered up prayers and supplication, with strong crying and tears." Heb. v: 7.

We have seen that the habits and customs of the Egyptians, must have been a trouble to Joseph, when he found himself a stranger there. But, how much more it must have been to Jesus, when he found himself living in this sinful world of ours! This world is strange to us when we first begin to live in it. But then *we* have never lived before at all. We have no recollection of another home, for we never had any. But it was different with Jesus. He had always lived in heaven, "in the bosom of the Father," before he was born as an infant in Bethlehem. And he never could forget that heavenly home. There, everything is holy, and good, and bright, and beautiful, and happy. There the angels had always worshiped him, and waited on him. What a change it must have been for him to come and live in this dark and sinful world! We can imagine how Joseph must have felt in Egypt when he thought of that quiet and lovely home, where he had lived with his father Jacob in "the vale of Hebron." But we cannot tell how Jesus felt, while a stranger in this world of sorrow, when he thought "of the home over there," that blessed heavenly home where he had dwelt with his father and the holy angels. This was part of the trouble that came to him from the mission on which he was sent. We see how much there was in their sufferings in which Joseph and Jesus were alike. But there was one thing here in which they were *not* alike. Joseph did not know the meaning of his sufferings, or what they were intended to lead to. But Jesus knew what his sufferings were for. He "saw the end from the beginning." The apostle Paul tells us, in speaking of Jesus—"of the joy that was set before him." Heb. xii: 2. This was the joy of saving the souls of his people. He knew what he was suffering for, and this made him so willing to bear it. And so we see that Joseph and Jesus were alike in this—they both had trouble from the mission on which they came.

But, in the next place, Joseph's trouble brought him to GREAT HONOR, *and here too he reminds us of Jesus.*

One morning Joseph came out of his room in the prison and met two of his fellow-prisoners. One of these was the chief butler of Pharaoh, king of Egypt. Our word butler, comes from an old English word that means a bottler, or one who has charge of bottles. And this butler of Pharaoh was one who had the charge of his wines and silver plate. The other fellow-prisoner of Joseph was the chief baker of Pharaoh. These two men had offended their master, and he had sent them both to prison. Joseph had become well acquainted with them there. When he met them on this morning he was surprised to find them looking very sad. He asked what was the matter. They said they had each dreamed a dream during the night, and they were in trouble because they could not tell the meaning of it. Joseph said that God knew the meaning of all dreams. Then he asked them to tell him their dreams. They did so: and at once he explained to them what their dreams meant. Within the next three days, what Joseph had said about those dreams came to pass. Pharaoh hanged the chief baker on a tree, but restored the chief butler to his office. We can read about this in the fortieth chapter of Genesis.

When Pharaoh sent for the butler, he came to say good-by to Joseph, before leaving the prison. Joseph asked him to remember him, his fellow-prisoner, when in prosperity, and try to get him out of prison. He promised to do so: "*yet did not he* remember Joseph but forgot him."

Then two long and weary years of prison life passed slowly away; and it must have seemed to

Joseph, as if not only the chief butler, but every one else in the world had forgotten him. But it was not so. God had not forgotten him. He never forgets his people. The time for Joseph's release came at last.

One night Pharaoh king of Egypt dreamed a dream. It was a very singular one. He dreamed it twice on the same night. When he woke in the morning he was in great trouble about his dream. He told it to his family and friends, but they could not explain it. He sent for all the wise and learned men in Egypt to help him, but none of them could tell what that strange dream meant. The whole palace was excited about it. The king was in great distress. And then the chief butler remembered Joseph, and those dreams in the prison, which he had explained so correctly. He went straight to the king and told him about it. Immediately the king sent a messenger to the prison with an order for Joseph the Hebrew to come directly to the palace. He shaved off his beard, for the Egyptians never let their beards grow except as a sign of mourning: and it was not considered proper for a person wearing a beard to come into the presence of the king. Then he laid aside his prison dress, and putting on suitable raiment, appeared before

the king. He told Joseph his dream. See Gen.
xli: 15-36. At once God enabled him to understand its meaning and explain it to Pharaoh.
He showed the king how a dreadful famine was
coming upon Egypt, which would last for seven
years; and how God had sent this dream that
Pharaoh might know of the coming trouble,
and prepare to meet it. And then, in a very
modest way, Joseph ventured to suggest to
Pharaoh what he had better do, so as to be
ready for the years of famine when they
came.

While Joseph was saying all this Pharaoh
looked on him with surprise and wonder. Then
he turned to his princes and said,—"Can we
find such a man as this, in whom the spirit of
God is?" And at once he made Joseph the
prime-minister, or highest officer of the kingdom. And Pharaoh said to Joseph, "See, I have
set thee over all the land of Egypt." And Pharaoh took off his ring from his hand, and put it
on Joseph's hand, and arrayed him in garments
of fine linen, and put a chain of gold about his
neck; and he made him ride in the second
chariot that he had; and they cried before him,
"Bow the knee: and he made him ruler over
all the land of Egypt."

How wonderful this was! Here we see how Joseph's trouble brought him to the prison, and then the prison brought him to the palace. In one day, by a single step, this great change was brought about. When the sun arose on the morning of that day, its light streamed through the iron bars of his window, and shone on Joseph, a poor forgotten prisoner; but before that same sun went down, its evening rays were shining on Joseph as he stood in the presence of Pharaoh, or as he walked up and down the halls of his splendid palace a "ruler of all the land of Egypt."

And how beautifully this part of Joseph's history reminds us of Jesus! The trouble he had to bear for us brought him to the grave. That was the dark prison in which our Joseph was bound. But from the grave he rose to life again. And thus he ascended into heaven, and took his seat at the right hand of God, and was made the ruler of our world, and of *all* worlds, as Joseph was made ruler over all the land of Egypt. See how the apostle Paul speaks of the matter. "He took upon him the form of a servant—and humbled himself, and became obedient unto death, even the death of the cross. Wherefore God also hath highly exalted him, and given him a name which is above every other name: That at the name of Jesus every knee should bow, of things in heaven, and things on earth, and things under the earth: And that every tongue should confess that Jesus Christ is Lord, to the glory of God the Father."   Phil. iii: 7-12.

Joseph rose from the prison to the palace of Pharaoh, to be ruler of all the land of Egypt. Jesus rose from the grave to the palace of the Great King of heaven, and to be ruler of all the universe.

When Joseph became rich and great he used his power for THE GOOD *of his brethren, and this is the last thing in which he reminds us of Jesus.*

We cannot stop now to speak of all the interesting matters connected with Joseph's history. How busy he was during all the seven years of plenty!   Now, they are over, and the years of famine begin.   The famine is not confined to Egypt.   It reaches to Canaan.   Jacob and his family are suffering for bread.   They hear that there is corn in Egypt, and the old patriarch Jacob, sends his ten sons down there to buy corn.   They appear before Joseph.   He knows them, but they know not him.   What a meeting that must have been!   What strange thoughts of the past must have come rushing into Joseph's mind! But we cannot dwell on these things. And then how he accuses them of being spies: how he keeps Simeon as a prisoner, or a pledge for their return: how he charges them to bring their younger brother with them, when they come again: how his heart melted when he saw his brother Benjamin: his plan to keep Benjamin as a slave: the noble conduct of Judah in offering to take Benjamin's place: how Joseph could refrain no longer then, but made himself known unto his brethren: what a touching scene it was, and how bewildered and overwhelmed with astonishment they must have been when Egypt's great ruler stood up in the midst of them, and speaking no longer by an interpreter, but in their own Hebrew tongue, said: "I am Joseph, your brother, whom ye sold into Egypt; doth my father yet live?" and how he wept and they wept, and then how lovingly he kissed his brethren;—all this we must pass over.

We come now to speak of what he did for his father, and his brethren,—the wagons that he sent them, loaded with the good things of Egypt. Now he brings them all down from Canaan. He places them in the best parts of the country. He gives them freely of all the good things that Egypt brought forth. And he finds positions of honor and profit for his brethren in the service of the king. Pharaoh told Joseph to do this, and it was all for Joseph's sake. "And Pharaoh spoke unto Joseph saying, Thy father, and thy brethren are come unto thee: The land of Egypt is before thee: in the best of the land, make thy father and thy brethren to dwell." Gen. xlvii: 5, 6. And so Joseph used his high office and the great influence he had with Pharaoh for the benefit of his brethren.

And how wonderfully Joseph's history points us to Jesus here! We are told that "God hath put all things under his feet, and made him head over all things to his church," or his people. Ephes. i: 22. He is exalted to the right hand of God, on purpose to give his people whatsoever they may need. Joseph had charge of all the treasures of Egypt, and when the hungry, starving people came to Pharaoh for bread "he sent them to Joseph." We read in Gen. xli: 56,—"*And Joseph opened all the storehouses unto the Egyptians.*" And in the same way, Jesus, our glorious Joseph, opens all the storehouses of heaven: and when poor, perishing souls are hungering for the bread of life, God sends them to Jesus. The apostle Paul says, "My God shall supply all your need according to his riches in glory by Christ Jesus." Phil. iv: 19. And when we ask for grace, and blessing, and any good thing from God, we must ask these things—"for Jesus' sake." This is the golden key that unlocks the treasury of heaven. Jesus said to his disciples,—"Whatsoever ye shall ask the Father, *in my name*, he will give it you." John xv: 16.

"For Charlie's Sake."—Some years ago, during the war, there was a Judge who felt great interest in the welfare of the suffering soldiers. He had a dear boy of his own in the army, and this made him feel the greatest sympathy for the soldiers. But one time he was very busy in studying out an important law case that was coming before him to be tried. And while he was thus engaged, he made up his mind not to be interrupted by any persons begging for help.

One day, during this time, a poor soldier came into his office. His clothes were torn and thin, and his face showed that he was suffering much from sickness. The Judge went on with his work, pretending not to notice him. The soldier was fumbling in his pockets for a good while, and then, seeing that he was not welcome, he said in a disappointed tone, "I *did* have a letter for you, sir." The judge made no answer. Presently the soldier's thin, trembling hand pushed a little note along the desk. The Judge looked up, and was going to say, "I am too busy now to attend to anything of this kind." But just then his eye fell on the note, and he saw the handwriting of his own son. In a moment he picked it up and read thus:— "Dear Father: The bearer of this note is one of our brave soldier boys. He has been dismissed from the hospital, and is going home to die. Please help him, in any way you can, for Charlie's sake."

What a change those few lines made in that father's feelings towards the poor soldier! "Come into the house my friend," he said. "You are welcome to anything we have." Then a good meal was prepared for him. He was put to sleep in Charlie's bed. He was dressed in some of Charlie's clothes, and money was given him to take him home in comfort. All this was done "for Charlie's sake." And so when we ask anything for Jesus' sake, God, our heavenly Father, will surely give it to us, if it be well for us to have it.

And thus we have Joseph and Jesus compared. Joseph was sent on a mission by his father; and so was Jesus. Joseph's mission was to show his father's love; and so it was with Jesus. Joseph's mission brought him into trouble; and so did that of Jesus. Joseph's trouble brought him to great honor; and so it was with Jesus. When Joseph became rich and great, he used his power for the good of his brethren; and this is just what Jesus is doing all the time. And so, when we read the sweet story of Joseph, let us never forget to think about Jesus, and to love and serve him for all that he has done for us.

The Flight Into and Return from Egypt

And when they were departed, behold, the angel of the Lord appeareth to Joseph in a dream, saying, Arise, and take the young child and his mother, and flee into Egypt, and be thou there until I bring thee word: for Herod will seek the young child to destroy him. When he arose, he took the young child and his mother by night, and departed into Egypt. And was there until the death of Herod: that it might be fulfilled which was spoken of the Lord by the prophet, saying, Out of Egypt have I called my son. Then Herod, when he saw that he was mocked of the wise men, was exceeding wroth, and sent forth, and slew all the children that were in Bethlehem, and in all the coasts thereof, from two years old and under, according to the time which he had diligently enquired of the wise men. Then was fulfilled that which was spoken by Jeremy the prophet, saying, In Rama was there a voice heard, lamentation, and weeping, and great mourning, Rachel weeping *for* her children, and would not be comforted, because they are not.— *St. Matt. ii: 13–18.*

NOTE BY THE ARTIST

In a journey such as this, i. e., the return from Egypt, it would be contrary to Eastern use and wont that the woman should ride while her husband walked. Only in cases of sickness or infirmity would such a departure from ordinary custom be deemed justifiable. In Syria infants are usually carried by their mothers upon the hip, older children upon the shoulder, as in the picture. The border of Egypt was not much more than one hundred miles from Bethlehem. Egypt was the common asylum for distressed inhabitants of Palestine, from the times of Abraham and Jeroboam, and Jeremiah.

9

CHRIST THE PROPHET LIKE MOSES

MOSES told the children of Israel that God would raise up to them a prophet like unto him. Deut. xviii: 15. And Christ was the person to whom he referred when he said this. Moses was one of the greatest men of whom we read in the Old Testament. Like Joseph, he spent the greater part of his life in Egypt. The history of Moses is very different from that of Joseph in many respects. But there is one thing in which the lives of these two good and great men are much alike: they both have many things in them that remind us of Jesus. We have seen how beautifully Joseph and Jesus may be compared together. And we may do the same here. The life of Moses is full of illustrations of the character and work of Christ. Moses knew this, and he told the children of Israel so when he said to them,—"The Lord thy God will raise up unto you a prophet, from the midst of thy brethren, *like unto me.*" This promise, or prophecy, refers to Christ. And it gives us an interesting subject of Bible study. It leads us to think of our blessed Saviour as "the prophet like Moses."

A prophet is one who speaks for another, and especially who speaks for God. And this is what Christ was sent into our world to do. He was to be a prophet. He was to come into our world on purpose to speak to us for God. And so the apostle Paul says, that, "God, who spake in time past unto the fathers by the prophets, hath in these last days spoken unto us by his Son." Heb. i: 1, 2.

It is true that Jesus was to be a prophet. And we are not only told this about him, but we are told also what sort of a prophet he was to be. He was to be "*a prophet like Moses.*" And the question we must try and answer now is this: What are some of the things in which Jesus was a prophet like Moses? I say *some* of them; for we cannot speak of them all. If we should try to count them, we should find that there are thirty or forty things in which Jesus was like Moses.

I will speak of only *five* of these things. Moses was exposed to great danger at the time

of his birth; and it was the same with Jesus—
*and so we may begin by saying that Jesus was like
Moses in*—THE DANGER ATTENDING HIS BIRTH.

Pharaoh, the king of Egypt, tried to kill Moses
as soon as he was born. The children of Israel
were increasing so fast that he began to be afraid
of them. Then he gave orders to have all the
male children of the Israelites thrown into the
river. And this was the law of Egypt at the time
when Moses was born. Exod. i: 22. The mother
of Moses hid her child for three months. What
an anxious time she must have had during those
months! No doubt the officers of Pharaoh who
had been appointed to execute this cruel law
were going about, all the time, hunting for
young children, whom their fond mothers were
trying, in one way or another, to save alive.
How many a piercing shriek would be heard, in
the homes of the Israelites, as some poor mother
pressed her darling to her bosom, in the vain
attempt to prevent it from being torn from her
embrace, and cast into the river Nile! How
often the heart of Jochabed, the mother of
Moses, must have sunk within her as she heard
these cries! She knew well what they meant.
And she knew not how soon her own time
might come to utter such a cry. We can well

imagine how she would be afraid to close her eyes at night, lest while she slept her babe might be snatched away from her. Every sound would alarm her. Every strange step she heard approaching her humble dwelling would fill her with fear. How could she tell but it might be one of the king's officers whose business it was to take the tender little ones from the arms of their weeping mothers and toss them into the river! How she would tremble when the child cried! and what anxious efforts she would make to hush the babe, lest the sound of its little voice might be heard by the men whom she so much dreaded! All this was kept up for three long, and weary months. And then she felt that this would not do. She saw "that she could no longer hide him." Exod. ii: 3. Perhaps the officers had become more strict in their searches. At any rate, Jochabed was convinced that something else must be done, or else she would soon lose her child. No doubt she had had many a long and anxious talk with her husband about what was the best thing for them to do. And many an earnest prayer, we can well imagine, they offered together that God would guide them, and show them what to do, in order to save their darling little one from death.

And then came the thought of the ark of bulrushes. We are not told who first suggested this idea. It is not said that an angel came from heaven and told Jochabed about this. And yet this thought must have come from above. We know how true it is, as one of the beautiful Collects in the Book of Common Prayer expresses it, that it is—"God from whom all holy desires, all *good counsels*, and all just works do proceed." And the hymn we sometimes sing, teaches the same thing when it leads us to look up to God, and say:

> " Thou all our works in us hast wrought,
>   Our good is all divine ;
>   The praise of every holy thought,
>   And righteous word is thine."

We are very sure it was God who put the thought of the ark into the mind of Jochabed. We are told that "she took for him an ark of bulrushes, and daubed it with slime and pitch." Exod. ii: 3. The "bulrush" was a reed that grew along the borders of the Nile in those days, though it is seldom found there now. It is called the papyrus reed. The ancients made out of this reed the material they used for writing upon. And it is from this that our word "paper" comes. This reed was much used by

the Egyptians for making baskets and vessels
for sailing on the river. The prophet Isaiah
speaks of large vessels, even such as were used
for going to sea, as being made out of the same
reeds, here called bulrushes. Is. xviii: 2.

It is likely that the mother of Moses had a
basket made of these bulrushes, which was in
use about the house. She made it waterproof
by covering it with bitumen, or as it says in the
Bible by "daubing it with slime and pitch."
Then she took her darling babe, and gently laid
him in the ark, kissed it, and covered it up.
We are not told about this in the history, but
we may be pretty sure that she kneeled down
beside that ark, before taking it out of her house,
and asked God to take care of it, and to keep it
from all harm. And then she carried it to the
river, and laid it down among the flags and
rushes that grew along the banks of the river.
But she left Miriam, the sister of Moses, a short
distance off, to keep watch over the ark, and see
what might become of it.

What an exposed position it was for that poor
child to be in! How many dangers there were
that might have befallen it! But God was taking
care of that helpless babe; and when he takes
care of us we are always safe. It was so with

that ark of bulrushes. We are not told how long Miriam had to wait and watch there. But at last she heard the sound of approaching footsteps. A company of females is drawing nigh. When they come in sight she recognizes one of them as the daughter of Pharaoh, king of Egypt. The others are her attendants. As they come nearer, the princess sees something floating on the water. She sends one of her maids to fetch it. The ark is uncovered, and the babe weeps. The turning point in that child's history has come. The future of his history all depended on how that young princess should feel towards him. Who could tell what her feeling would be? When she saw it, and knew it to be one of the Hebrew's children, suppose that she had said: "My father has made a law that all the male children of these Hebrew slaves shall be put to death. This is one of them. According to that law this child must die. Take it out of the ark, and throw it into the river." She might have done this. It would have seemed most likely that she would do it. But she did not. The hearts of all people, we know, are in God's hand, and "He can turn them, as the rivers of water are turned." The heart of this young princess was in God's hand.

He wished her to be kind to that helpless little one, and he turned her heart towards him in kindness. And it is interesting to notice how God did this.

When the ark was uncovered in the presence of the princess, we are told that—"the babe wept." Exod. ii: 6. A weeping babe is always a touching sight. To see the big tears filling its little eyes, and rolling down its innocent cheeks is enough to melt any heart. Here it melted the heart of Pharaoh's daughter, and opened it in tender love and kindness towards this helpless babe. She resolved to adopt it as her own child, and take it home to her palace. And so, we may say that this baby's tears made its fortune.

And here Josephus, the Jewish historian, mentions a little incident, which is not told in the Bible history. He says that Pharaoh's daughter tried first to get an Egyptian nurse to take care of the child; but though she tried several, one after another, the child would not go to any of them. And then he says, Miriam came up and offered to get a Hebrew nurse. She was told to go and get one. She brought the babe's mother. He went to her in a moment. "And Pharaoh's daughter said unto her, take this child, and nurse it for me and I will give thee thy wages." How happy Jochabed must have felt when she took her darling child home that day! Before she had nursed her babe with fear and trembling. Now all her fear was gone. Until then there had been the danger of death attending him ever since he was born. But now that gracious God to whose kind care she had committed him had heard her prayer. The king's daughter had become his friend, and he was not only saved from the fear of death, but a good education and everything he could need was freely provided for him. And here we see what the danger was that attended the birth of Moses. And if we turn now from Moses to Jesus, we find that there was danger attending his birth too. And so he was like Moses in this respect.

Herod was king in Jerusalem at that time. When he heard that a child had been born who was to be "king of the Jews," he was afraid he might lose his kingdom. So he resolved to kill this child. He tried first to do it by getting the wise men to come back and tell him where he might find the young king. God would not let them do this, but "sent them back to their own country another way." When Herod found

this out, we are told, that "he was exceeding
wroth, and sent forth, and slew all the children
that were in Bethlehem, and in all the coasts
thereof, from two years old and under, according to the time which he had diligently inquired
of the wise men." Matt. ii: 16. In this way he
thought he would surely secure the death of
the young child that he feared so much. And
the child Jesus would certainly have been killed
by this cruel order of Herod if God had not
interfered to take care of him. But this was
just what God did. He sent an angel to tell
Joseph "to take the young child and his mother,
and flee into the land of Egypt." Matt. ii: 13.
Joseph did this. And so, when Herod's soldiers
were making bloody work among the babes of
Bethlehem, the infant Saviour of the world was
far away out of their reach, safe in the hiding-
place that God had found for him in Egypt.
And so we see how well Jesus might be called
"the prophet like Moses" when we think of the
danger that attended his birth.

*In the second place, we see how Jesus was like
Moses, in his*—PREPARATION FOR HIS WORK.

There were two parts in the preparation that
Moses went through: one was *a preparation of
privilege,* the other *a preparation of trial.* The

preparation of privilege was what Moses had when he was "called the son of Pharaoh's daughter." He lived in the palace of Pharaoh. He had the best education that could be had anywhere in those days. The Egyptians were the most learned people in the world at that time. People, in other parts of the world, who wished to get a good education went to Egypt and studied there. The best schools or colleges were there. They had the best teachers or professors. It was necessary for Moses to have the very best education that could be had in order to fit him for the great work he was to do. The Bible teaches us that God "makes all things work together for good to them that love him." Rom. viii: 28. And we have a beautiful illustration of the way in which he does this when we see how God made use of Pharaoh's cruel law to kill the Hebrew children, and of the ark of bulrushes in which the mother of Moses placed him, in order to secure for him the privilege of living in the palaces of Egypt, and of getting all the knowledge that Egypt could give. And we know that "Moses was learned in all the wisdom of the Egyptians, and was mighty in words and deeds." Acts vii: 22. This was the preparation of privilege that Moses had to fit him for the important work to which he was called.

And Jesus was "a prophet like Moses" in this respect.   He had a preparation of privilege too. Before he came into the world to be our Saviour, it had been his privilege to live, not in such palaces as those of Egypt, but in the great palace of the King of heaven.   He had been "in the bosom of the Father."   John i: 18.   He had had a share "in the glory of the Father before the world was."   John xvii: 5.   The words that he spake, and the works that he did while in our world, he tells us were only "what he had seen with his Father."   John viii: 38.   If Moses needed great wisdom and knowledge to fit him for the work he had to do, how much more did Jesus need?   Yes, and how much more did Jesus have?   He could say "all power in heaven, and on earth is given unto me." Matt. xxviii: 18.   And "in him are hid all the treasures of wisdom and knowledge."   Col. ii: 3.   The work he came into the world to do was a wonderful work, and what a wonderful preparation he had for doing it!

But then, in addition to this preparation of privilege, Moses had also *a preparation of trial* to fit him for his work.

When Moses was forty years old he had finished his education in Egypt. He knew a great deal about other things, but very little about himself. He thought he was old enough and wise enough to do anything. Without asking God's help, or direction, he undertook to deliver the children of Israel out of Egypt. But he made a great mistake. He got into trouble and had to flee from Egypt. He had much more to learn before he would be fit for the work God meant him to do. He had been to school for forty years in Egypt, with princes and great men. Then God sent him to school forty years more in the wilderness. There he was alone with his sheep. In that school God was his teacher. He taught Moses many valuable lessons about himself and his own heart. And Moses learned these lessons well. And so after his preparation of trial was finished, God appeared to him at the burning bush. There he gave Moses his commission, and the directions that he needed about the way in which he was to deliver the children of Israel out of their house of bondage in Egypt.

And Jesus was like Moses, too, in this respect. He had a preparation of trial to go through. The thirty years that he spent in Nazareth, working as a carpenter, with Joseph his supposed father, were all years of trials to him. And when these years were over, he went into the wilderness to be tried or tempted there. God was pleased to make use of Satan himself to prepare our blessed Saviour for his work. A part of the preparation of trial through which he passed was what took place when he was "led up of the spirit into the wilderness, to be tempted of the devil." Matt. iv: 1. And the apostle Paul shows us what a useful preparation this was, when he says, in speaking of Jesus: "For in that he himself hath suffered being tempted, he is able to succor them that are tempted." Heb. ii: 18. And so we see how truly Jesus might be called the prophet like Moses. He was like him in his *preparation for his work.*

But in the third place, Jesus was "the prophet like Moses," on account of the many—MIRACLES—*that he did.*

Moses performed more miracles than any other person of whom we read in the Old Testament. He was commanded to carry a rod in his hand, and when he was going to work a miracle he was to wave this rod, and then God caused the miracle to take place. These

Jesus at Nazareth

But when Herod was dead, behold, an angel of the Lord appeareth in a dream to Joseph in Egypt, Saying, Arise, and take the young child and his mother, and go into the land of Israel: for they are dead which sought the young child's life. And he arose, and took the young child and his mother, and came into the land of Israel. But when he heard that Archelaus did reign in Judea in the room of his father Herod, he was afraid to go thither: notwithstanding, being warned of God in a dream, he turned aside into the parts of Galilee. And he came and dwelt in a city called Nazareth: that it might be fulfilled which was spoken by the prophets, He shall be called a Nazarene. And the child grew, and waxed strong in spirit, filled with wisdom: and the grace of God was upon him.—*St. Matt. ii: 19–23; St. Luke ii: 40.*

NOTE BY THE ARTIST

"Ain Miryam," or Mary's Well, is one of the sites of whose authenticity there can be no reasonable doubt. It is the only public fountain in Nazareth, and thither must the Virgin Mother and her child have proceeded daily to draw water for the household. In the well has been followed the outlines of the arch left by the Crusaders, but with an earlier style. The habit of carrying the water-jars and other burdens on the head gives all the women of Palestine a notably graceful carriage.

10

10

miracles were not intended for show, but for use. God never does anything for show. There is always something useful in whatever he does. The first miracle that Moses did was intended to be a proof to Pharaoh that God had sent Moses to deliver the Israelites. When he appeared before Pharaoh and asked him to let the children of Israel go forth from their captivity in Egypt, it is not surprising that Pharaoh was unwilling to do what Moses asked. The Israelites were then a nation of slaves. For many years they had been brickmakers and builders for the Egyptians. They had been doing all kinds of hard work, and doing it at very small cost. It seems that they got nothing for their labor but a bare support. This must have made their labor very profitable to the Egyptians. Therefore it was not likely Pharaoh would be willing to let them go if he could help it. So when Moses came before Pharaoh, and told him that he came with a message to him from "the Lord God of the Hebrews;" and this message was that he must let the children of Israel go, Pharaoh would very naturally be ready to say, "Well, but how do I know that this is true? What proof can you give me that you come from God?" Then the first miracle that Moses had to work came into use. When God gave him his commission, at the burning bush, he prepared him to meet this very difficulty.

Moses had his brother Aaron with him. He carried the rod. Moses told him to throw it on the ground before Pharaoh, and it became a serpent. Pharaoh called in the magicians of Egypt to see what they could do. They with their enchantments did that which looked like the same kind of miracle; but it was not. They could not make real serpents out of wooden rods as Moses did; but they contrived to do something that seemed to be a miracle, just as we have seen a conjuror like Signor Blitz do many things which appeared like miracles, but were not so. The serpent into which the rod of Moses was turned swallowed up the other serpents. And when he took it by the tail, and it became a rod again, the magicians had lost their rods. But Pharaoh would not believe Moses; nor do what God wanted him to do. He thought that Moses was only an abler magician than the others. He said he would not obey God.

And the other miracles that Moses was commanded to do were all intended to make Pharaoh obey God, and let the children of

Israel go. Here we see a great contest going on. God is one of the parties in this contest, and Pharaoh is the other. God's command to Pharaoh is,—"Let my people go." Pharaoh's answer to this command is,—"Who is the Lord, that I should obey his voice to let Israel go? I know not the Lord, neither will I let Israel go." Exod. v: 2.

And now we are to look on and see how this contest ends. Moses is before us with his rod. He begins by asking Pharaoh to let Israel go. Pharaoh says,—"I will not do it." Then Moses waves his rod. Immediately all the water in the river Nile, and in the wells of Egypt is turned into blood. No one can drink it, and all the fish in the river die. Exod. vii: 19-25. The Lord told Moses that "He would execute his judgments against the gods of Egypt." Exod. xii: 12. We may keep this in mind as we speak of the different plagues with which Moses, in God's name, punished the Egyptians. They were dependent on the annual overflowing of the river Nile for the fertility of their land. On this account they regarded that river with feelings of reverence. They worshiped it as a god. To have the water of their favorite river turned into blood therefore must have

been particularly painful and distressing to
them. It would cause the Egyptians to turn
away with disgust and loathing from the river
which they always looked upon as a sacred
object. They were made to feel that here was
one of their gods who had no power at all
against the Lord God of the Hebrews.

By this miracle God punished the Egyptians
for two sins of which they had been guilty.
The had been *guilty of idolatry* in worshiping
this river. They had boasted that by reason of
this river they were independent of the rains of
heaven. They had paid to this senseless stream
the homage and worship that were due only to
the God of heaven. They praised that river for
the blessings which they owed only to God.
We need not wonder then that in beginning
his work of judgment on the Egyptians God
should lay his hand of power first upon the
river which they had made an idol, and should
make it indeed a plague and a curse to them.
Good old Bishop Hall says, "that when we put
anything in the place of God, he will surely
cause us to suffer most through that very thing."

And then God punished the *cruelty*, as well
as the idolatry of the Egyptians by sending this
plague upon their river. They had stained the

waters of that river with the blood of the Hebrew children; and now all its streams were filled with blood as if to remind them of their sin.

A second time Moses waved his rod, and a multitude of frogs came up from the river Nile. They cover the land. In the homes of the poor; in the dwellings of the rich; in the palace of the king they are found. Kitchen, and parlor, and bed-chamber, and every place is filled with their polluting presence. This must have been, in some respects, a more distressing plague than the former one. If the people found the sight of the blood in their river painful and disgusting to them, they could go away from the river to their homes, and there they would be free from this annoyance. The river could not follow them. But the frogs could, and did. They were everywhere. It was impossible to get away from them. Imagine yourself there. If you walk in the road, you cannot see the ground for the frogs. If you enter the house to sit down frogs cover the chair you would sit upon. You go to the closet for something to eat; the frogs are over everything. You take a cup to get a drink of water, and there is a frog in it. You begin to kill them; but for every one you kill, a dozen more come to take its place. Worried out with the sight of them, you go to your bed for rest, and lo! the bed is full of frogs! You give up in despair. The sight, and the slime, and the stench of these vile creatures are about you wherever you go.

And the frog was another of the sacred animals of the Egyptians. To think of worshiping a frog! Yet they did. They had a frog-headed goddess. And such was the reverence with which these creatures were regarded in some parts of Egypt that dead frogs were embalmed, and buried, and monuments erected to them. In this plague of the frogs we see another judgment executed on the gods of Egypt.

Again the rod is waved, and the flies come in endless swarms. The people cannot breathe without taking them into their mouths and nostrils. Our English Bible speaks of this plague as consisting of "swarms of flies." In the Hebrew Bible the word "flies" is left out. It only speaks of "swarms," without saying what they were. In speaking of this David says,—"He sent divers sorts of flies among them, which devoured them." Ps. lxxviii: 75. In Exod. viii: 24, we are told that "the land was corrupted by reason of the swarms of flies." And as these swarms not only filled the air, but covered the ground, it is supposed that the beetle was found among them. This creature is an object of great dislike to persons generally. It is considered as a nuisance or plague wherever found. But in Egypt beetles are always numerous, and very offensive. They devour everything that comes in their way, even clothes, books, and plants. They even inflict severe bites on the inhabitants of the land. And yet the beetle was considered as a sacred creature by the Egyptians. It was held in high honor, and was also an object of worship among them. Pliny, the historian, says, —"A great portion of Egypt worship the beetle as one of the gods of the country." One of the ways in which they honored it was by having its figure engraved on seals, or cut in stone; it was used in all kinds of ornaments, and particularly in rings and necklaces. They not only worshiped the beetle when alive, but they embalmed it when dead, and embalmed beetles and beetles cut in stone are often found among the ruins and in the tombs of Thebes. In the British Museum, in London, there is a colossal figure of a beetle cut in greenish colored granite. And to have these sacred beetles made their tormentors, to see them invading their homes and covering the public roads in such numbers that "the land was corrupted by them," must have been a very painful thing to the Egyptians. They were obliged to crush under their feet and to sweep away from their homes and streets and to look with abhorrence on the very creatures they had been accustomed to worship. And when they knew that it was the great being whom the Hebrews worshiped, who was thus "executing judgment on the gods of Egypt," they must have felt that "there was none like unto the God of Israel."

Once more the rod is waving. And now a terrible disease called murrain, breaks out among the cattle of Egypt. Suddenly it seizes on the horses, the asses, the camels, the oxen, and the sheep. None escape the disease. No remedy for it is known. Its work is quickly done, and the end of the matter is that "all the cattle of Egypt died: but of the cattle of the children of Israel died not one." Exod. ix: 1-7.

And now for once the rod is laid aside. Instead of a rod Moses takes a handful of ashes from the furnace. He stands before Pharaoh and scatters the ashes towards heaven. The effect is wonderful. At once boils, painful and burning, break out upon men, and upon beasts throughout all the land of Egypt. The beggar on his dunghill, the prince in his palace, and the king upon his throne, all are covered with boils. Who can tell the misery that Egypt had to bear from this plague?

Again Moses stands before Pharaoh. Still the demand is, "Let my people go." Pharaoh refuses. Again that wondrous rod is waved. And now a terrible hailstorm bursts upon the land. This is something before unknown in Egypt. The loudest thunder roars through the sky. Flash after flash of the sharpest lightning blazes out from the storm-cloud, and runs in streams of fire along the ground. The hail rattles terribly against the roofs of the dwellings. Plants are killed; trees are broken; and men and cattle found in the field are destroyed all through the land. Egypt looked like a ruined country when that tremendous hailstorm had swept over it. Exod. ix: 13-35.

Again Moses appears before Pharaoh. Again that mighty rod is raised. Slowly the man of God waves it. And see, yonder comes a cloud. It comes not like the cloud which the prophet's servant saw rising from the sea, but from the way of the wilderness. How fast it comes! How rapidly it grows broader, and deeper, and darker! And now it covers the heavens. It shuts out the light of the sun. It is a cloud of locusts. This is one of the most dreadful evils known in that part of the world. The prophet Joel gives the best description of one of these locust-plagues that ever was written. He says, —"A fire devoureth before them; and behind them a flame burneth: the land is as the garden of Eden before them, and behind them a desolate wilderness; yea, and nothing shall escape them. The appearance of them is as the appearance of horses; and as horsemen, so shall they run. Like the noise of chariots on the tops of mountains shall they leap, like the noise of a flame of fire that devoureth the stubble, as a strong people set in battle array. Before their face the people shall be much pained: all faces shall gather blackness. They shall run to and fro in the city; they shall run upon the wall, they shall climb up upon the houses; they shall enter in at the windows like a thief. The earth shall quake before them; the heavens shall tremble: the sun and the moon shall be dark, and the stars shall withdraw their shining. And the Lord shall utter his voice before his army: for his camp is very great." Joel ii: 3-12. Such an army of locusts, invaded Egypt when Moses waved his rod. They devoured every green thing that the hail had left. The land seemed to be utterly destroyed. And yet Pharaoh would not let the people go.

Once more Moses appears before the king. He repeats God's command to let the people go. Again it is refused. Again the rod is waved, when lo, a horrible darkness settles down upon the land. It was utterly unlike the gloom of our darkest nights. There was something in it solemn and awful. We are told it was "a darkness that might *be felt*." I suppose this means a darkness attended by thick clammy fogs and vapors, so heavy and damp that the people could put forth their hands and feel them. Not only was the light of the moon and the stars hidden, but it is most probable that neither lamps nor fire would burn. Only such a state of things would explain what we read in Exod. x: 23, where it says that—"They saw not one another, neither rose any from his place for three days." What dreadful days those must have been! I suppose that David refers to these days of fearful darkness when he says that God "sent evil angels among them." Ps. lxxviii: 49. They would terrify the people by strange and fearful noises, that would seem ten times more alarming on account of the darkness. And when we think of all this suffering we see what a terrible thing it is to fight against God!

And now we come to the last and most wonderful work that God did in Egypt through Moses. This was the most terrible of all. It took place on what is called the night of the Passover. The Israelites had been told to kill a lamb for every family. The blood of this lamb was sprinkled on the posts of their doors. Then, as the night went on, the people were holding a feast. It was called "the feast of the Passover." This was the most memorable night the children of Israel had ever passed through. It was the night of their great deliverance from the bondage of Egypt. The 12th chapter of Exodus gives a full account of the way in which they were to keep the feast that was connected with their deliverance on this night. In the 24th verse of this chapter God said to them— "Ye shall observe this thing for an ordinance to thee and to thy sons forever." And in the 42d verse, we read—"It is a night to be much observed unto the Lord for bringing them out from the land of Egypt: this is that night of the Lord to be observed of all the children of Israel in their generations."

There were two reasons why God commanded the Israelites to keep this "feast of the Passover" every year.   One of these reasons had to
do with the *past*.   It was to help them in keeping alive in their hearts a grateful memory of
God's wonderful mercy in delivering them from
Egypt.   No nation in the world ever had such
a deliverance as this.   And when the pious Jew
kept this feast, from year to year, in the way
that God commanded, it would do him a great
deal of good.   It would remind him of the
state of bondage in which his forefathers had
been held.   It would make him feel that God
had been a great friend to him and to all his
people.   It would teach him how he owed all
he had in the world to the God who had been
the deliverer of their nation; and how he ought
to show his gratitude to him by loving him
with all his heart, and serving him faithfully
all his days.

But then there was another reason why God
commanded the Israelites to keep this feast.
This had to do with the *future*.   There was a
sort of prophecy in this feast, and the solemn
sacrifice connected with it.   It was all intended
to point to Christ.   It was a figure or type of
him.   The lamb that was slain, at this feast,

pointed to Christ, the spotless, perfect Lamb of God who was to be slain on Calvary. The protection which the Israelites had on that night from the death of their first-born, by means of the blood sprinkled on their doors, pointed to that deliverance from everlasting death which all the people of Christ have through faith in the blood which he shed for them on the cross. And the land of promise—that "good land, flowing with milk and honey"—which the Israelites were to have as their possession, when the long journey was ended, on which they started that night, pointed to that better land—that heavenly Canaan—which Jesus has gone to prepare for his people, and to which he will lead all who believe in him.

When Jesus was on earth, he met his twelve disciples, on the night in which he was betrayed, in an upper chamber in Jerusalem, to celebrate for the last time, the Jewish Passover. The feast was kept in the usual way. And when it was ended, Jesus established another solemn service, which was to take the place of the Jewish Passover, and to be observed by his friends and followers to the end of the world. While they lingered round that table, we read, that—"Jesus said unto them, 'with desire I have

Jesus in the Midst of the Doctors

Now his parents went to Jerusalem every year at the feast of the passover. And when he was twelve years old, they went up to Jerusalem after the custom of the feast. And when they had fulfilled the days, as they returned, the child Jesus tarried behind in Jerusalem; and Joseph and his mother knew not *of it*. And when they found him not, they turned back again to Jerusalem, seeking him. And it came to pass, that after three days they found him in the temple, in the midst of the doctors, both hearing them, and asking them questions. And all that heard him were astonished at his understanding and answers. And when they saw him, they were amazed: and his mother said unto him, Son, why hast thou thus dealt with us? behold, thy father and I have sought thee sorrowing.—*St. Luke ii: 41–43, 45–48.*

NOTE BY THE ARTIST

Jesus is here represented, making no display of his own learning, but as a searcher after brighter wisdom than he as yet possessed. For this purpose, having doubtless exhausted such means of knowledge as could be provided in his provincial home, he eagerly seized the opportunity afforded by his first visit to Jerusalem to attend the theological lectures delivered in one of the schools of the Temple, adjoining the Court of the Gentiles. Amongst the doctors of the law who "were astonished at his understanding and answers" may have been the aged Hillel and his great rival Shammai, the Rabban Simeon, Jonathan ben Uzziel, and others whose names are associated with this period of brilliant rabbinical learning. In default of definite knowledge regarding the architectural style of the interior of the Temple, its leading features, in this as in other pictures, are, to a great extent, adopted from those of "the Dome of the Rock" which occupies the same site.

11

11

desired to eat this passover with you before I suffer. For I say unto you, I will not any more eat thereof, until it be fulfilled in the kingdom of God.' And he took bread, and brake it, and gave it to his disciples, saying, 'Take, eat: this is my body which is given for you. Do this in remembrance of me.' Then he took the cup, and when he had given thanks he gave it to them, saying, 'Drink ye all of this; for this is my blood of the New Testament, which is shed for you, and for many, for the remission of sins; do this, as often as ye shall drink it in remembrance of Me.' "

Thus was instituted the Sacrament of the Lord's Supper. The solemn scene connected with it was one of the most interesting and important that ever took place in the history of our world. It marked the passing away of the Jewish Passover and the religious system that was connected with it, and the introduction of the Christian Sacrament of the Lord's Supper, which was to take the place of the service established in Egypt, and which had been kept up for so many hundred years. And the meaning of this solemn sacrament, and the feelings we should have when celebrating it, and the benefit we should pray to derive from it, are

beautifully set forth in the following extract
from the Communion service of the Episcopal
Church:

"All glory be to thee, Almighty God, our
heavenly Father, for that thou, of thy tender
mercy, didst give thine only Son Jesus Christ
to suffer death upon the cross for our redemp-
tion; who made then—(by his one oblation of
himself, once offered)—a full, perfect, and suffi-
cient sacrifice, oblation, and satisfaction for the
sins of the whole world: and did institute, and
in his holy gospel command us to continue, a
perpetual memory of that, his precious death,
and sacrifice, until his coming again.

"Grant us therefore, gracious Lord, so to eat
the flesh of thy dear Son Jesus Christ, and to
drink his blood, that our sinful bodies may be
made clean by his body, and our souls washed
through his most precious blood, and that we
may ever more dwell in him, and he in us."

And now, after this long digression, let us go
back to the memorable scene we are contem-
plating in Egypt. The night goes on. The
solemn hour of midnight comes. And now,
the angel of the Lord passes over all the land of
Egypt, and by one fearful blow of his unseen
sword smites the first-born, both of man and

beast, in every family. At the same moment, from the palace of the proud king to the hut of the poorest family in the land, *there is one dead in every house.* And then what a wail of woe was heard! A cry of sorrow and anguish arose in Egypt, and sounded through the land. Such a cry was never heard before or since. Then the haughty Pharaoh felt that he could contend no longer. God had conquered. The king gave up. He sent for Moses and Aaron and told them to take their people and be gone! And then what is called the Exodus, or the going out, took place, and the Israelites began their grand march from Egypt to the promised land.

Such were some of the miracles that Moses wrought in Egypt. And when we think of the miracles that Jesus did, we see how truly he was "the prophet like Moses" in this respect. Indeed his miracles were much more numerous than those of Moses. It is easy to count up the miracles of Moses; but none can tell how many the miracles of Jesus were. What numbers of them are mentioned in the gospels! And these, we are told, were only a small part of them. In the last verse of the gospel of St. John we find a statement made that may very well be brought in here. That loving disciple of Jesus had written his long, full history of the wonderful words that Jesus had spoken, and the wonderful works that Jesus had done. But then he wanted us to understand that he had not attempted to give a full report of all the gracious words that had fallen from his lips, or all the great miracles that had been performed by his hands; and so he winds up his gospel in this way:— "And there are also many other things which Jesus did, the which, if they should be written every one, I suppose that even the world itself, could not contain the books that should be written."

And then the miracles of Jesus were not only more in number than those of Moses but, we may well say that they were *better* miracles. The first miracle of Moses turned water into blood; but the first miracle of Jesus turned water into wine. John ii: 1-12. The miracles of Moses are all called plagues. They were sent on purpose to plague and punish the Egyptians. But the miracles of Jesus were all blessings to the people. They were designed only to help and comfort the people, and to do them good. He healed the sick; he opened the eyes of the blind; he unstopped the ears of the deaf; he made the lame to walk; he raised the dead to life again, and so "went about doing good," in every possible way.

And thus we see how well he might be called "the prophet like Moses," on account of the miracles that he performed.

In the next place, Moses gave the people the— LAWS, OR COMMANDMENTS—*of God, by which they were to be governed; and Jesus was "the prophet like Moses" for this reason also.*

A great part of the books of Exodus, of Numbers, and Leviticus is filled with the different laws that Moses gave to the Israelites to show them how they were to offer their sacrifices, and conduct the other parts of the worship of God.

And then Moses went up to the top of Mount Sinai, and was there forty days with God, learning all the things that he was to tell the people. A thick cloud covered the top of the mountain when God came down upon it. And while God was speaking to all the people the words of the ten commandments, from the midst of that cloud, the lightnings flashed, and the thunders roared, and the angel's trumpet sounded long and loud! That was the grandest and most awful scene that our earth has ever witnessed.

Then God wrote the words of those commandments with his finger, on two tables of stone, and gave them to Moses. He brought them in his hands to the people, when he came down from the mountain. They were put into the Ark of the Covenant, as soon as it was made, and kept there for hundreds of years, until Nebuchadnezzer came, and carried the Israelites captives to Babylon.

And Jesus spent all the years of his ministry on earth, in teaching the people the laws or commandments by which they were to live and be guided in all their conduct. Let us just look for a moment at two of the laws or rules that Jesus gave to his people, by which they were to regulate their conduct. In the sermon on the mount he said: "*Whatsoever ye would that men should do to you, do ye even so to them.*" Matt. vii: 12. This is called "the golden rule." And well it may be so called! It is related of a great emperor, that when he first heard of this law of Christ, he was so much pleased with it, that he caused it to be printed in letters of gold, and hung up in his palace.

And then on another occasion Jesus said to his disciples: "*A new commandment I give unto you, that ye love one another.*" John xiii: 34.

How beautiful this is! There are many wise and excellent things among the laws that Moses gave to the Israelites; but there is nothing in them to be compared to either of these golden rules that Jesus gave to his disciples. What a bright and blessed world this will be when people learn to live according to these beautiful laws of Jesus! Our earth will be like heaven then. These are the rules by which Jesus lived himself. And in doing this he has left us an example that we should follow his steps. And we must do this, if we wish to be truly the friends and followers of Jesus; for it is said, "Let this same mind be in you, that was also in Christ Jesus:" and, "If any man have not the spirit of Christ he is none of his."

And so when we think how Jesus gave his people the laws and commandments of God, by which they were to govern their lives, we see how truly he may be called—"the prophet like Moses."

But in the last place Jesus might well be called "the prophet like Moses" because of—THE BLESS-INGS—*he obtained for his people.*

Moses was the means of securing a great many blessings for the people of Israel. It would take a long time to tell of them all. But chief among these are *five* that we must speak about.

The first of these was—*guidance.*

When Moses led the children of Israel up out of Egypt, the way to the promised land by which they were to go lay through "a waste howling wilderness." There were no turnpike roads through that wilderness. No fingerboards, in that desert region, pointed out the way to the land of Canaan. People can travel through that wilderness now, by the help of a compass, with its friendly finger, pointing always towards the North. But Moses had no compass. It had not been invented then. And as neither Moses, nor any one among the Israelites knew the way through that wilderness, we see, at once, how much they needed guidance. It was a blessing of the very first importance to them. Moses, with all his learning would never have been able to guide his people through the wilderness if God had not come to his help. He promised to send an angel to be their guide. Exod. xxiii: 20. And with this angel he sent a cloudy pillar which rested over the Tabernacle. In the day time it looked like one of those white fleecy clouds that we see floating in the sky; but at night it turned red, and looked like a flaming fire.   We can read the account of this in Numb. ix: 15-23.   When this cloud stood still the Israelites were to stay in their encampment.   But when the cloud rose, and began to move, that was the sign for them to strike their tents, and travel on after the cloud.   This cloud was like the tent in which the guiding angel had his abode, or like the chariot in which he rode, as he led the Israelites on through the wilderness.

Of course Moses did not make this cloud come; but God directed Moses to tell the people about it; and so we may speak of this guiding cloud as one of the blessings which Moses obtained for them.

And Jesus is like Moses in this respect, because he secures the blessing of guidance for his people.   This world is like a wilderness.   There are many paths through it, yet among them all there is but one that will lead us to the heavenly Canaan.   We need a guide to show us this path.   And Jesus is the only one who can be our Guide.   In one place in the Bible he promises to guide us with his eye.   Ps. xxxii: 8.   In another, he promises to guide us with his counsel.   Ps. lxxiii: 24.   We are often like a traveler when he comes to a place where the road he has been traveling branches off into two or three roads. There are no finger-boards to show where they lead to, and he cannot tell which is the right road to take. And then it is that we need guidance. There is a sweet promise in God's word for just such occasions as these. In Isaiah xxx: 21, God says, *"And thine ears shall hear a word behind thee, saying, This is the way, walk ye in it, when ye turn to the right hand, and when ye turn to the left."*

Here is an illustration of one of the ways in which God sometimes guides his people, or makes them hear the voice which is to tell them what to do.

Some years ago there was a good minister of the Gospel in England, whose name was the Rev. John Fletcher. When he was a young man he was very anxious to join the army, and go to South America. His friends had consented for him to go. They had secured an appointment for him in the army. His passage was taken; the vessel was ready to start; but the very morning on which he was to have sailed, the servant in bringing his breakfast to him, stumbled and spilled a tea-kettle of boiling water over him. This scalded him so severely that he could not go. It was a great disappointment to him. But *that* was God's way of telling him not to go in that vessel; for the vessel was lost, and all on board perished.

There is another sweet promise in the Bible about the guidance. In Prov. iii: 6 we read, "In all thy ways acknowledge him, and he shall direct thy paths." There is both a duty and a privilege in this passage. The duty is that we should acknowledge God in all our ways. This means that we should ask him to help and guide us in all that we do. It is said of the late excellent Bishop Heber, who wrote the beautiful missionary hymn, "From Greenland's icy mountains," that he never went on a journey, never began to write a sermon or to read a book, or do anything without first offering up a prayer for God's guidance and blessing. Thus he acknowledged God in all his ways. And this is what we are to do. This is the duty we are taught here. And then there is a privilege as well as a duty in this passage. The privilege is that if we so acknowledge God, he will guide us, or "direct our paths." Here is an illustration of both the duty and the privilege spoken of in this passage.

An artist painted a picture of a little child in the dress of a pilgrim. He is walking slowly along a path. This path has on each side of it a dreadful precipice. The edges of these precipices are hidden from view by means of beautiful flowers that are growing there. Behind the child is an angel. His face is full of tenderness and love. His hands are resting lightly on the shoulders of the child, to keep him in the centre of the path. The child has closed his eyes that the sight of the flowers may not tempt him into danger. He is walking carefully along, feeling and following the gentle touch of the angel that is leading him. He acknowledges the angel by following his touch; and while he does this the angel "directs his paths."

We each have such an angel. Ps. xxxiv: 7. Hebs. i: 14. These angel-touches are very soft and gentle. We must watch for them carefully, and follow them faithfully, if we wish to be led in safety along the dangerous path that we have to travel. Moses obtained for the Israelites the blessing of guidance, by means of the fiery cloudy pillar. Jesus is like Moses because he secures guidance to each of his people, by his word, and spirit, and providence.

Another blessing that Moses obtained for the children of Israel was—SHELTER.

David tells us that God—"Spread a cloud for a covering." Ps. cv: 39. The wilderness through

which the Israelites journeyed for forty years
was a wide waste of barren sands. The sun
shines there with intense heat. The sand gets
very hot, and reflects, or throws back, the heat
which the sun pours down upon it, so that
travellers there are, as it were, between two
fires. What they greatly need is shade. But
there are no trees there to give them shade.
God knew what the Israelites would need in
their long journey through that terrible wilderness, and so "he spread a cloud for a covering."
Take, for instance, a great oak tree. See what
a sturdy, solid trunk it has! And above see
how its branches spread themselves out on
every side! In the hot summer days what a
pleasant shade those branches make! God has
spread them out for a covering. And when we
see the little birds lodge among those branches,
and the cattle gather under the cool refreshing
shadow which the branches make, we have a
good illustration of the way in which God
spread out a cloud for a covering to his people
Israel, as they journeyed over the burning sands
of the desert. Let us suppose that the cloud
which guided the Israelites stood over the
Tabernacle, in the shape of a great column,
like the trunk of a tree. And then, let us

suppose that the top of that column spread itself out, on every side, like the branches of a tree. We have only to think of that out-spreading cloud as reaching to the ends of their encampment, and then, in the form of that vast shadowy tree, we can see how it was that the cloud that guided them was the same that shel-tered them, during all the wanderings of their long pilgrimage.

This was a great blessing. And Jesus may well be called a prophet like Moses, because he secures to his people, as they journey through the wilderness of this world, blessings well represented by the comfort and refreshment which the Israelites found from that sheltering cloud in the wilderness.

We find many illustrations of this in the Bible. There is Job in the midst of his long, dark trial. His children are all dead. His property is all lost. His health is gone. A horrible disease has broken out all over his body. His friends instead of comforting him only add to his misery by their unkind words. There is no prospect that anything but death will end his sufferings. And yet, in the midst of all this sorrow and trouble he could look up to God his Saviour, and calmly say,—"Though

The House in Nazareth

And he went down with them, and came to Nazareth, and was subject unto them: but his mother kept all these sayings in her heart. And Jesus increased in wisdom and stature, and in favor with God and man. And Jesus himself began to be about thirty years of age, being (as was supposed) the son of Joseph, which was *the son* of Heli.— *St. Luke ii: 51, 52; iii: 23.*

NOTE BY THE ARTIST

Beyond the fact that he was subject to his parents, that he grew in wisdom as he advanced in age, and that he was beloved by all who knew him, the picture illustrates all that we know of the life of Jesus until he attained the age of thirty years. He worked with Joseph as a carpenter at Nazareth, making the simple articles which comprise the furniture of an Eastern home, and, amongst other things, the primitive wooden ploughs still in use in all parts of Palestine.

12

12

he slay me, yet will I trust in him." What real comfort Job must have found in this shelter of which we are speaking!

David had many heavy trials to bear; and yet while bowed down beneath the burden of them he could say,—"The Lord is my refuge, and my fortress; my God; in him will I trust." Ps. xci: 2. And so sure was he of finding comfort in this shelter that when he thought of the heaviest trials that could possibly come upon him he said,—"Yea, though I walk through the valley of the shadow of death, I will fear no evil; for thou art with me; thy rod, and thy staff they comfort me." Ps. xxiii: 4.

How much comfort the prophet Isaiah must have felt in this shelter when he could speak thus beautifully about it: "A man shall be as a hiding-place from the wind, and a covert from the tempest; as rivers of water in a dry place, as the shadow of a great rock in a weary land. Is. xxxii: 2.

Here is an illustration of this sweet passage furnished by an incident that occurred not long ago:

A party of travellers in the desert were overtaken by one of those stormy winds that blows there, called a Simoom. The hot sands were driven fiercely along like blinding snow. Just before the wind reached its height the travellers came to a rude stone building, well protected with roof and doors. It had been built there by some charitable person on purpose to afford shelter to travellers from those terrible winds. With great joy the party rushed forward. They entered the building, closed the doors, and were safe. And so when the storms of sorrow and trouble, burst upon us in this world, if we are the friends of Jesus we shall find how true the words of Solomon are when he says,—"The name of the Lord is a strong tower; the righteous runneth into it, and is safe." Prov. xviii: 10. And then there is another sweet passage in which Jesus speaks of himself as the refuge of his people, and invites them to come and find shelter in him. In Is. xxvi: 20, he says,—"Come, my people, enter thou into thy chambers, and shut thy doors about thee: hide thyself as it were for a little moment, until the indignation (or trouble) be overpast."

When Shadrach, Meshach, and Abednego walked up and down amidst the burning fiery furnace, we are told that there appeared one with them "like unto the Son of God." This was Jesus. And it was the shelter he gave them which kept the fire from hurting them.

And when Daniel was thrown into the den of hungry lions, it was the shelter Jesus gave by his angel that shut the lions' mouths so that they did not hurt him.

And this shelter can protect those who seek it as well now as it did then.   Here is an illustration:—On board a British man-of-war there was but one Bible among seven hundred men. This belonged to a pious sailor who had made a good use of it.   He had read it to his comrades, and, by God's blessing on his labors, a little band of praying men was formed that numbered thirteen.   One day his ship was going into battle.   Just before the fight began, these thirteen men met together to spend a few moments in prayer.   They committed themselves to God's care, not expecting to meet again in this world.   Their ship was in the thickest of the fight.   All around them men were stricken down by death.   Two of these men were stationed with three others in charge of one of the guns.   The other three men were killed by a single cannon ball.   But there in safety stood the two praying men.   They had agreed that when the battle was over, those who might still be alive should meet if possible. They met soon after, and what was their joy to find the whole thirteen were there. Not one of them had even been wounded. What a blessed shelter it was that protected those men of prayer!

Jesus is the prophet like Moses, because he secures to his people the blessing of shelter.

But HEALING *was another blessing that God gave to the Israelites through Moses, and on this account, too, Jesus may well be called "the prophet like Moses."*

We read that as the Israelites were journeying through the wilderness at one place, when they were disobedient and rebellious, the Lord sent fiery serpents among them. These serpents bit the people. Their bite was poisonous. The wounds caused by them were very painful. A burning heat attended them which caused much suffering to those who were bitten. The physicians could not cure the bite of these serpents, and so great numbers of the people were dying from this cause. Then God told Moses to make a serpent of brass, and put it on a pole, and set up the pole in the midst of the encampment where everybody could see it. Then he was directed to tell the people to look at that serpent, and to assure them that every one who believed what God said, and looked to the serpent on the pole should live.

Moses does what God tells him. He makes the brazen serpent. He puts it on a pole. He sets the pole where it can easily be seen. And then he sends word to the bitten, suffering, dying people to look at this serpent and they shall be healed. And now, all through the encampment, how many eyes are looking towards that serpent! Some who have just been bitten look to the serpent, and are healed. Some who are so sick that that they cannot leave their beds are carried out of the tent, so that they can see the serpent. They look, and are healed. Others are so far gone that they are just about to die. They are not able to move. But kind friends gently turn their heads upon their pillows. Their dying gaze is directed to that wondrous serpent. Death is obliged to loose his hold upon them. Even *they* are healed, and restored to life.

This was the blessing of healing which Moses secured for the Israelites. And we know how beautifully Jesus made use of this incident to show that he was "the prophet like unto Moses." In John iii: 14, 15, Jesus says,—"*As Moses lifted up the serpent in the wilderness, even so must the Son of man be lifted up: that whosoever believeth in him should not perish, but have eternal life.*"

This is God's own illustration of Christ's healing power, and it is the best we can have. It shows us how souls bitten by the serpent, sin, are healed, and saved, by believing in Jesus, just as the bitten Israelites were saved by looking to the brazen serpent.

The Bible has a great deal to say about the wonderful healing power of Jesus. One of his special, peculiar names is made up in this way. He says of himself,—"I am the Lord that *healeth* thee." Exod. xv: 26. He tells us that this is the very work he was sent to do. "The spirit of the Lord is upon me, because he hath sent me to *heal* the broken-hearted." Luke iv: 18. How ready Jesus was to heal the sick when he was on earth. When the Centurion applied to Jesus to come and heal his servant who was sick of the palsy, his quick and loving answer was,— "I will come and heal him." Matt. viii: 7. Moses healed the Israelites of only one disease, and that was the poison of the fiery serpents. But how different it was with Jesus! When he was on earth we are told, that—"they brought unto him all sick people that were taken with divers diseases, and torments, and those which were possessed with devils, and those which were lunatic, and those that had the palsy; *and*

he healed them.''   Matt. iv: 24.   And his power
to heal is the same now that it was then.   Every
earthly physician does at times have some poor
sufferer come to him for healing, to whom, after
examining his symptoms, he is obliged to say
as he shakes his head, "My poor friend, I am
sorry to tell you that I can do nothing for you."
But Jesus, the heavenly healer, never says this.
He can *heal*, just as he can save, *"unto the uttermost.''*   Here is an illustration of what I mean:

"Some time ago," says a minister in London,
"a person called at my house, and requested me
to come and see a little girl, only seven years
old, who was very ill.   I went with the messenger who took me to the room where the
sick child was.   I sat down by her bedside, and
said: 'What do you want of me, my child?'

"'Well, sir,' she said, 'I wanted to tell you
something before I die.'

"'And are you dying, my dear?'

"'Yes, sir.'

"'And wouldn't you like to get well again?'

"'No, sir, please God.'

"'And why not?'

"'Why, sir, you see,' she said,—and remember
she was only seven years old,—'ever since I
became a Christian, I have been trying to get

father to go to church; and he won't go.   I do
so want him to hear the precious gospel! And
so if I die you will bury me, won't you, sir?'
I said, 'Yes, my darling.' 'Well, I've been
thinking if I die, father must go to the funeral;
and then you can preach the gospel to him;
and oh! sir, I would be willing to die *six times
over* that father might hear the gospel once!'
What wonderful love was in that dear child's
heart!

"Well, the little darling died; but just as she
was to be buried I was taken very ill, and could
not go to the funeral. This grieved me very
much. But God can always do his own work
without our help, as he did in this case. For,
not long after a rough fellow called on me. He
held out his hand, and said,—'You don't know
me, sir, do you?'

"'No, sir, I do not.'

"'Well, sir, I am little Mary's father. I heard
as how she said she would die for me six
times, if I could only hear the gospel once. It
nearly broke my heart. And now, sir, will you
tell me about this gospel, and what I must do
to be saved?'

"I told him about Jesus, and prayed with
him. He soon became a Christian, and is now

a useful member of the church. Jesus made use of the wonderful love of that dying child to heal and save her wicked father. It is all true as that sweet hymn says:

" Come ye disconsolate, where'er ye languish
    Come, at the feet of Christ fervently kneel;
Here bring your wounded hearts, here tell your anguish,
    Earth has no sorrow but Jesus can heal."

Another blessing that Moses procured for the Israelites in the wilderness was daily BREAD, *and for this reason, too, Jesus is properly called "the prophet like Moses."*

There was no bread to be had in that desert wilderness through which the Israelites were journeying. They numbered between two and three millions of people. They were to be forty years on their journey. Of course they were not travelling all that time; but they had to spend that time in the wilderness. To carry provisions with them for such a multitude, during so many years was simply impossible. It was absolutely necessary that they should be fed, yet they could only be fed by miracle.

And this was just the way in which God told Moses that he intended to feed them, as long as they were in the wilderness. He caused their bread to fall round about their tents every night, as gently as the dew falls on the grass. In the morning they looked out of their tents, and there lay the manna, as it was called, covering all the ground, as we sometimes see the hoar-frost on a fine winter's morning. They had nothing to do but go out and gather it before the sun rose. The Jewish measure called an omer, containing about three quarts, was the quantity allowed for each person in every family. The manna was a hard substance, in the form of small seeds, of a greyish-white color. It was ground, or pounded in a mortar, and then used, as we use meal, by baking it in cakes. The taste of it was like wafer cakes made with honey. All that was gathered in the morning had to be used before night. If they kept it till the next morning it bred worms and spoiled. They were not allowed to gather any on the Sabbath-day; and so, on the morning of every sixth day they were to gather a double quantity to last them over the Sabbath, and yet this never spoiled. God performed a special miracle every week, to show how much he regarded the Sabbath-day, and to teach them to regard it too. We can read about this in Exod. xvi: 14-36, and Numb. xi: 4-9. This manna is what David speaks of in one place as "bread from heaven," Ps. cv: 40,

and in another place as "angels' food." Ps.
lxxviii: 25. Thus we see that bread, or food for
the people, was one of the blessings that Moses
obtained for them.

And this points us to Jesus. He may well be
called "the prophet like Moses" on this account.
When he was on earth, he was talking to the
Jews one day about this manna which God
gave their fathers through Moses, and he said,—
"Your fathers did eat manna in the wilderness,
and are dead. I am the living bread which
came down from heaven: if any man eat of this
bread, he shall live forever." John vi: 49, 51.
"For the bread of God is he which cometh
down from heaven, and giveth life unto the
world." John vi: 33. He may well be called
"the bread of life," because he gives us all the
bread we have, both for our souls and bodies.
He is "The Lord" of whom David says that he
—"giveth food to the hungry." Ps. cxlvi: 7.
It is he who "giveth to all life, and breath,
and all things." Acts xvii: 25. It is he who
"openeth his hand and satisfieth the desire of
every living thing." Ps. cxlv: 16. It is he who
gives us this sweet promise,—"I will satisfy her
poor with bread." Ps. cxxxii: 15. He does
this in a common or general way by sending

rain and sunshine to make things grow in plenty, for our use. And then he sometimes does this in a special, particular way by sending bread to the needy when they call upon him for it. Here is an illustration of what I mean:

Some time ago, a good Christian man was living among the hills of Scotland. He was very poor, but so good that every one who knew him loved and honored him. One winter there was a violent snow-storm. The wind was high, and drifting snow blocked up the roads, and quite covered the humble dwelling of poor Caleb, as this good man was called. Fot three days he had been unable to go out and get food for himself and family. They were in great need, and had prayed earnestly for relief. A gentleman living in that neighborhood, who knew Caleb well, awoke suddenly one night. It seemed as if a voice was calling to him which said—"*Send provisions to Caleb.*" He thought little of it, but turned on his pillow and went to sleep again. Again the voice seemed to sound in his ears—"*Send provisions to Caleb.*" Again he slept. A third time the call came. Then he arose hastily, dressed himself, called up his servant, and told him to harness the horse, while he filled a basket with provisions of all kinds. "Take this basket to Caleb," said he, "and if he asks who sent it, tell him *it comes from God.*" The servant did as he was bidden. A path was made through the snow. The basket of food was left at Caleb's cottage; and he and his family received it with hearty rejoicings. They felt sure that it was food from heaven, just as truly as the manna was in the wilderness, on which the Israelites lived. Moses secured the blessing of bread for the Israelites in the wilderness, and Jesus is " the prophet like Moses" because he secures this blessing both for the bodies and the souls of his people.

The only other blessing, of which I will speak, that Moses secured for the Israelites was WATER, *and Jesus is like Moses in this respect, too.*

Bread is a necessary thing; but unless we have water also it will be of little use. However much bread we may have, still we should soon die unless we can get a good supply of water. The manna which God sent in such a wonderful way to his people in the wilderness, could have done them no good unless he had been pleased to send them water also. God knew this. When Jesus was on earth he said to his disciples,—"*Your heavenly Father knoweth what things ye have need of, before ye ask him.*" Matt. vi: 8.   And so God told Moses to take in his hand the rod so often used and smite a great rock in Horeb, and that he would cause water enough to come forth from the smitten rock, to supply and satisfy the thirsty and suffering people.   Moses obeys God.   He takes the rod.   He stands before the rock and smites it, it opens; and out gushes a torrent of clear, cool, sparkling water.   What a blessing this was to them!   What music there was in the sound of the rushing waters!   How loud the shout of joy they raised!   And then, how eagerly they stooped down to bathe their heated brows in the flowing stream, and to comfort themselves with good, long draughts of its refreshing waters!

And very beautifully all this points us to Jesus.   This smitten rock with its outgushing water is a figure of Christ.   When the apostle Paul is speaking of this to the Corinthian Christians he says that the Israelites "all drank of that spiritual Rock that followed them; and *that Rock was Christ.*"   I. Cor. x: 4.   What he means to say is that this rock, with its outflowing stream of water was intended to be a type,

The Baptism of Jesus by John

Then cometh Jesus from Galilee to Jordan unto John, to be baptized of him. But John forbad him, saying, I have need to be baptized of thee, and comest thou to me? And Jesus answering said unto him, Suffer *it to be so* now: for thus it becometh us to fulfil all righteousness. Then he suffered him. And it came to pass in those days, that Jesus came from Nazareth of Galilee, and was baptized of John in Jordan. And straightway coming up out of the water, he saw the heavens opened, and the Spirit like a dove descending upon him. And there came a voice from heaven, *saying*, Thou art my beloved Son, in whom I am well pleased. Now when all the people were baptized, it came to pass, that Jesus also being baptized, and praying, the heaven was opened. And John bare record, saying, I saw the Spirit descending from heaven like a dove, and it abode upon him. And I knew him not: but he that sent me to baptize with water, the same said unto me, Upon whom thou shalt see the Spirit descending, and remaining on him, the same is he which baptizeth with the Holy Ghost. And I saw, and bare record that this is the Son of God.—*St. Matt. iii: 13–15; St. Mark i: 9–11; St. Luke iii: 21; St. John i: 32–34.*

NOTE BY THE ARTIST

The traditional site of the Baptism in Jordan, about six miles from Jericho, is here accepted and represented.

13

13

or shadow, of Christ and his work.   The bless-ings of that salvation which Jesus brings are often in the Bible compared to water.   Look for a moment at some of these passages.   It is Jesus who is speaking, by the prophet, when he says,—"I will pour water upon him that is thirsty, and floods upon the dry ground."   Is. xliv: 3.   It is he who gives this sweet promise: —"I will give waters in the wilderness, and rivers in the desert, to give drink to my people, my chosen."   Is. xliii: 20.   And it is he who sends out this precious invitation,—"Ho, every one that thirsteth, come ye to the waters." Is. lv: 1.   Here is the New Testament form in which Jesus puts this Old Testament invitation: "If any man thirst, let him come *unto me*, and drink."   John vii: 37.

Jesus gives the water of salvation to his people for two purposes: one for *cleansing*, the other for *comfort*.

The prophet Zechariah was speaking of Jesus when he said, "In that day there shall be a fountain opened for sin, and for uncleanness." Zech. xiii: 1.   This fountain was opened when from the wounded side of Jesus, as he hung upon the cross,—"There came out blood and water."   John xix: 34.   And it is this "blood of

Jesus Christ which cleanses us from all sin."
I. John i: 7. God compares this blood to water,
on account of its cleansing power, when he says,
—"Then will I sprinkle clean water upon you,
and ye shall be clean from all your filthiness:
and from all your idols, will I cleanse you."
Ezek. xxxvi: 25.

A poor soldier, wounded in one of the battles
of the Crimean war, threw himself on the
ground to die. "Oh! for a drop of water!" he
exclaimed. "There's not a drop in my can-
teen," said one of his comrades. "What can I
do for you?" "Bill," said the wounded man,
"open my knapsack, and get my Bible, and let
me have a drop of water from the well of salvation."

His comrade did so. He was led to open at
the first chapter of the first epistle of St. John,
which contains that sweet passage about the
cleansing blood of Christ. As he stopped reading, his friend said,—"Ah! Bill, that's it. What
could poor sinners like you and me do without
that cleansing blood? I shall never get back
to old England, but thank God, I shall go to a
better country, through the cleansing blood of
Christ. O, surely if ever the Bible was written
for any man, it was written for the poor soldier!"

But Jesus gives the water of salvation to *comfort* his people, as well as to cleanse them. When he was on earth, he said,—"Whosoever drinketh of the water that I shall give him, shall never thirst; but the water that I shall give him, shall be in him, a well of water springing up into everlasting life." John iv: 14. What a comfort to have a well of water like this springing up in our own hearts! People think it a great comfort to have a well of water on their place, or near their door; and verily it is so. But this is nothing compared to the well of water which Jesus opens in the hearts of his people. There is enough in this to make any one happy. God meant it to make us happy; and happiness follows wherever this water of salvation flows.

Here is an illustration of what I mean·

A Prussian nobleman who did not believe in God, nor in the Bible, once overheard a little girl singing one of her sweet hymns. He was much moved by the gentle tones of her voice. As he came near he saw tears upon her cheeks, as though she had been weeping. "Why are you crying as you sing?" he kindly asked. "Oh! it is because I'm so happy," said the little girl.

"But why do you weep if you are happy?"
"I love Jesus so," she said, "that I was crying
with joy."

"But where is Jesus?" asked the nobleman.
"In heaven."

"How can he do anything for you, if he is
in heaven? He cannot give you clothes, and
playthings, as your parents and friends do."

"Oh! yes! he can do a great deal for me. He
comes into my heart, and makes me happy."

"Nonsense!" said the nobleman. "This is
all nonsense."

"Oh! no, no, sir; indeed it is not nonsense,"
said the little Christian. "Nonsense wouldn't
make any body as happy as I am. But I know
it's true what the Bible tells me about Jesus. I
believe it, *and it makes me glad.*"

The nobleman turned away. He felt that
this child had a great blessing which he had
not. And that was true. Jesus had opened
this well of water in her heart, and it gave her
comfort to which he was a stranger. He was
led to seek that little girl's Saviour. And soon
the well of water was opened in his heart that
made him happy too.

We have written of five blessings which God
gave to the Israelites through Moses. He gave

them *guidance,* and *shelter,* and *healing,* and *bread,* and *water.* And Jesus is the prophet like Moses, because he gives such blessings to his people.

And we have seen that there were five things in the history of Moses on account of which he might truly say, when referring to Christ, "a prophet shall the Lord your God raise up unto you *like unto me.*"

These were *the danger attending his birth: his preparation for his work; the miracles he did; the laws he gave them; and the blessings he secured for them.* Five words contain it all—*birth— preparation—miracles—laws, and blessings.*

THE JEWISH TABERNACLE A FIGURE OF CHRIST

ONE observes that when a great temple, or an important building of any kind is to be put up, before the laborers begin their work, the architect, or chief builder, makes a plan of it. This plan is drawn with great care. It shows what the length, and breadth, and height of the building are to be. The doors, and the windows, and the different parts of the building are particularly described in this plan.

The Tabernacle which Moses built for the Israelites, while they were encamped at the foot of Mount Sinai, was one of the most interesting and important buildings ever erected. And one thing about it that helped to make it such was that God was the architect, or chief builder of it. He drew the plan of it. Before Moses began to build this Tabernacle, God called him up to the top of Mount Sinai. He was there for forty days with God. During those days God showed him the plan, or model of the Tabernacle which he was to build, and told him how every part of it was to be made. After showing him all this, before Moses came down from the Mount, God said to him: "See thou make all things according to the pattern showed to thee in the Mount." Heb. viii: 5. Exod. xxv: 40. And if God felt such an interest in this Tabernacle, and took so much pains about it, certainly it is worth while for us to study it carefully, and try to find out what it was intended to teach.

The apostle Paul tells us that this Tabernacle was a figure, or type, of Christ. He means by this, that God intended it to be an illustration of the character and work of Christ. He drew the plan of it, and had it built in such a way as would be best adapted to show, both to Jews and to Gentiles, what Christ was to be, and what he was to do for his people.

And in studying what we find written in the Bible about the Jewish Tabernacle, there are two things that it is very important for us to understand; one of these is,—*What the Tabernacle was;* the other is,—*What the Tabernacle taught.*

Now let us try and see if we can get a clear idea of *What the Tabernacle was.*

A plain and simple description of it is what I will now try to give.

Let us picture that we see a large space of ground enclosed or shut in by a kind of fence. At the further end of this enclosure is a building covered over with curtains. *That* is the Tabernacle with its enclosure. Now, let us suppose that you and I, with a company of half a dozen friends, were living at the time when Moses built the Tabernacle in the wilderness. We have heard about that strange building. We feel a great desire to see it. We have a week's vacation, and conclude to spend this time in visiting the encampment of the Israelites in the wilderness, and getting a good look at the Tabernacle. And here some wise boy will be ready to ask,—"Ah! but how are you going to get there? I should like to know." Never mind about that. When people go off on fancy journeys, mountains and oceans to be crossed and other difficulties are nothing to them. Let us suppose that we have arrived at the edge of the great encampment of the Israelites. There it is spread out for miles before us. We can tell where the Tabernacle is by the white, fleecy cloud that hangs over it. We make our way through the encampment. We inquire for

Moses, the great leader of this host. We pay our respects to the venerable man, and ask permission from him to visit and examine the wonderful structure built under his direction. He receives us very cordially, and tells us we are welcome to go through the Tabernacle and look at every part of it. It is against the law, indeed, to let strangers enter this Tabernacle, but he will make an exception in our case. Moses very kindly calls one of the Levites, and puts us in his charge, with directions to explain every thing to us. We make our grateful acknowledgments to the great Law-giver, and begin our examination of the Tabernacle.

We may suppose that it is one of the sons of Levi who is to be our guide. He is an amiable, obliging, intelligent young man, whom we may call Shelumiel. Our starting point is from the tent of Moses. This was always pitched directly in front of the entrance to the court of the Tabernacle, on the east side of the enclosure.

Before starting, our friend Shelumiel calls our attention to the broad open space lying between the Tabernacle enclosure and the encampment of the Israelites.

"Notice this wide space," he says,—"It is two thousand cubits, or three thousand feet, or rather more than half a mile wide. If you go to the corner of the enclosure and look along the right hand, or north side of it, you will see the same space there. If you walk round to the back of the enclosure, or the west side of it, you will find the same space there; and if you continue your walk along the south side, coming back to the point from which you started, you will find that there is the same broad space all round the enclosure, on every side. As we go on journeying through the wilderness," says Shelumiel, "every time the Tabernacle is set up again we are commanded to have this same broad space around it on every side."

"Shelumiel," says one of our company, will you please tell us what this is for? Why is there always to be this wide distance kept up between the enclosure of the Tabernacle, and the encampment of the people?"

"It is," says he, "because Jehovah, the God of Israel, dwells in the Tabernacle. He is a great and holy God. The angels of heaven veil their faces when they bow down before him. And when his people come near to worship him, he would have them do it with reverence and godly fear. And this broad space all round the place where he dwells is to teach the people reverence."

"And now, come, my friends," says Shelumiel, "and let us enter the court of the Tabernacle. There is only one way of entrance. This is directly behind the tents of Moses and Aaron, our great leaders. Look at the three central pillars, in the front of the enclosure. The curtains between them are not fastened, like all the rest of the curtains which make the fence of the enclosure, but are so arranged that they can be drawn aside. Let us draw these curtains to one side, and enter the enclosure. Now we are within the sacred place. Here let us stand a moment and look around. This enclosure is what is called 'the Court of the Tabernacle.' It is in the form, you see, of an oblong square. This means a square that is longer in one direction than in the other. The length of this court, from front to back, or from east to west is one hundred and seventy-five feet. Its breadth from north to south is eighty-seven feet and a half, and its height eight feet and a half. And just see how this enclosure is made. The fence that encloses it, or separates it from the space outside, is formed by curtains of fine linen, hung on pillars. These pillars are not round, but flat. They are made of a hard kind of wood, like box-wood, and known

as acacia wood. Every board or pillar is over-
laid with brass, and furnished at the bottom
with fillets, or tags, or thick points like a finger.
These are made to fit into sockets of brass,
placed on the ground. Each board or pillar,
when set up, is strengthened by stays or ropes
on both sides of it. These ropes reach from
the top of the board, and are fastened to stakes
driven into the ground. There are twenty of
these boards, or pillars, along each side of the
enclosure, with ten in the front and ten at
the further end. Between these boards, or
pillars, are hung linen curtains, which form
the walls of the enclosure, or 'the Court of the
Tabernacle.'

"And now," continues our friend Shelumiel,
"as I have told you how this enclosure is formed,
please take a good look at it, and notice what
there is in it. Observe that there are three
things in this enclosure. The first of these, or
the one nearest to us, is that square thing, made
of brass. It looks like a great box, with a pole
or staff on each side of it. That is the brazen
altar. There the morning and evening sacrifice
is offered up every day. Beyond this you see a
large round thing, something like a great basin.
That is called the brazen laver. It is kept filled

with water all the time, for the priests to wash their hands and feet in, as they engage in the service of God in the Tabernacle. And the building you see, beyond the brazen laver, is the Tabernacle itself, the holy place where God dwells, and from which he speaks to us from time to time through his servant Moses.

"Look at the appearance it presents from the outside, before we enter to see what there is within. Notice that it is of the same general shape as the enclosure in which it stands. Its length is forty-five feet, its breadth and height each fifteen feet. It is always made to stand facing the east. The two sides and the west end of the Tabernacle are composed of boards, of acacia wood, covered all over with pure gold. There are twenty of these boards on each side, and eight at the west end. There are no boards at the front of the Tabernacle. That end is all covered by curtains. The only entrance to it is by drawing aside one of those curtains. Each board has two tenons, or pieces of the board about as thick as a finger, made to fit into sockets. Each board has also five rings or staples through which bars are put for the purpose of steadying the whole building. There is no roof to the Tabernacle, as you see. Its only covering

Jesus Led of the Spirit Into the Wilderness

Then was Jesus led up of the Spirit into the wilderness to be tempted of the devil. And Jesus being full of the Holy Ghost returned from Jordan, and was led by the Spirit into the wilderness. Being forty days tempted of the devil. And in those days he did eat nothing: and when they were ended, he afterward hungered. And the devil said unto him, If thou be the Son of God, command this stone that it be made bread. And Jesus answered him, saying, It is written, That man shall not live by bread alone, but by every word of God. And the devil, taking him up into an high mountain, shewed unto him all the kingdoms of the world in a moment of time. And the devil said unto him, All this power will I give thee, and the glory of them: for that is delivered unto me; and to whomsoever I will I give it. If thou therefore wilt worship me, all shall be thine. And Jesus answered and said unto him, Get thee behind me, Satan: for it is written, Thou shalt worship the Lord thy God, and him only shalt thou serve. And he brought him to Jerusalem, and set him on a pinnacle of the temple, and said unto him, If thou be the Son of God, cast thyself down from hence. For it is written, He shall give his angels charge over thee, to keep thee. And in *their* hands they shall bear thee up, lest at any time thou dash thy foot against a stone. And Jesus answering said unto him, It is said, Thou shalt not tempt the Lord thy God. And when the devil had ended all the temptation, he departed from him for a season.—*St. Matt. iv: 1; St. Luke iv: 1-13.*

NOTE BY THE ARTIST

The part of the arid stony wilderness leading thence to the hill called Quarantania, the traditional scene of the Temptation. On the way, Jesus would approach, or cross, the brook now known as the Wady Kelt, which winds through this desert from a neighboring gorge until it reaches the Jordan.

14

14

consists of four different curtains which are spread over it for the protection of the building, and the furniture it contains.

"And now," continues our friend, "we are ready to enter this sacred building. I will draw aside the curtain, and very reverently we will enter. Here we are now within the most sacred building in the world. The Tabernacle is divided into two rooms. The one we are now looking at is the larger of the two. This is what is called the *Holy Place*. If you look up, you see overhead the first of the four curtains of which I have just spoken. It is covered all over with figures of angels, or cherubim, as they are called. They are worked, or embroidered on the curtain in blue, and purple, and scarlet. How beautiful it looks!

"Now, notice what there is in this holy place. Nearest to us, on the left, stands a golden candlestick. It has seven branches, and there is a light burning in each of them. On the opposite side you see a table with two rows of good sized loaves of bread upon it. This table is covered all over with gold, and it is called the table of shew-bread. Beyond this, and just in front of the curtain, which hangs down at the other end of the room, is a small altar. That is called the golden altar of incense. Here the priest burns incense, and its fragrance fills the Tabernacle. There is no light here but what shines from that candlestick, with its seven branches; and as you look around, you see how the golden sides of the Tabernacle glitter, and sparkle, as the rays from that sacred candlestick fall on them.

"Beyond that curtain, at the other end of this room," continues Shelumiel, "no one is allowed to enter, except the high-priest; and even he can only enter once a year. The law of this Tabernacle is that no stranger shall be allowed to enter it. But as our great law-giver, Moses, has made an exception in your case, my friends, I suppose I may be allowed to draw this curtain aside, and let you take a look at what is on the other side of it. There now, the curtain is removed. This part of the Tabernacle is called 'the Holy of the Holies,' or 'the most Holy Place.' There is nothing here but the Ark of the Covenant all covered with gold. On each end of the ark, you see is a golden angel, whose outstretched wings meet and form a sort of arch above. There, the cloud of God's presence rests; and from there, when he speaks to Moses, or the high-priest, his glory shines forth like the sun. As we stand here, and gaze on this solemn, sacred scene, how well we may take up the words which our father Jacob used at Bethel, when he had seen the vision of the ladder reaching up to heaven, and say: 'How dreadful is this place! This is none other than the house of God, and this is the gate of heaven!'"

Then our friend Shelumiel leads us out from the sacred place, to the spot where we first met him, and bids us "good-bye." We thank him heartily for this great kindness and then go back to our imaginary homes.

And now, I hope, we have a clear idea of the first thing of which we were to speak, *What the Tabernacle was.*

And this prepares us for the other point of which we were to speak; namely,—*What the Tabernacle taught.* It was a figure of Christ, and was intended to teach us some important lessons respecting him. We have in the Tabernacle a beautiful illustration of one of the precious names of Jesus our Saviour. Just before he came into our world, the angel Gabriel was sent to Joseph, his reputed father, to tell him about that wonderful child that was to be born unto Mary his wife. And this is what the angel said: "They shall call his name Emmanuel,

which being interpreted is, God, with us."
Matt. i: 23. This name is wonderful. It is
full of meaning. But many find it difficult to
understand its meaning. And so God ordered
the Tabernacle to be built in the wilderness,
that in it he might dwell among the people,
and thus be a figure or illustration to them of
the way in which Jesus now dwells in the hearts
of his people by faith. The Tabernacle was a
definition of this name—Emmanuel. As God
was present with the Israelites in the wilderness,
in the Tabernacle, so Jesus is present with his
people in this world. And as we study the
different parts of this Tabernacle we are taught
much that is interesting and profitable concerning the presence of Jesus with his people. The
Tabernacle taught four things about the presence of Christ in the hearts of his people.

*In the first place it taught that there was to be
—PARDON—connected with his presence.*

The brazen altar, or the altar of burnt sacrifice, was the part of the Tabernacle that taught
this lesson. That was the first thing one would
see on entering the Court of the Tabernacle.
Here the daily sacrifice was offered. Here the
blood of the slain animals was shed, that it
might be sprinkled both on the priests and on

the people. No one was allowed to enter the Tabernacle, or to worship God there till he had first been to this brazen altar, and had the blood of the sacrifice sprinkled upon him. And the great blessing represented by the shedding and sprinkling of the blood—was *the pardon of sin*. There was no power in the blood of those animals to put away sin, or to procure pardon. But it pointed to the blood of Christ, through which alone all pardon comes. And this is what the Apostle Paul teaches us, when he says that—"without the shedding of blood, there is no remission,"—(Heb. ix: 22), or no pardon. If Jesus had not shed his precious blood there never would have been any pardon for sin. But that blood *was* shed. And now there is pardon for all who repent and believe in him. His presence with his people is a pardoning presence. "He has power on earth to forgive sins." Matt. ix: 6. There is nothing we need more than pardon. We are born in sin. We sin every day, and we are always needing pardon. And it is a blessed thing to know that we can have this pardon at any time by seeking it in the right way. Jesus is—*"ready to forgive."* Ps. lxxxvi: 5. His promise is that—"He will *abundantly* pardon." Is. lv: 7.

Here is an illustration of the pardoning power of Jesus. It was told by a sailor who witnessed it, who was made a Christian by it, and afterwards became a chaplain.

"Our vessel lay at anchor," said he,—"off the coast of Africa. The yellow fever had broken out on board, and several of the men had died. It was my duty every morning to go through that part of the vessel used as a hospital, and see if any of the men had died during the night. One morning as I was passing through the sick ward, a poor fellow lying there, took hold of me with his cold, clammy hand. I knew him very well. He was an old shipmate, and one of the wickedest men on board. I saw in a moment that he had not long to live.

"'Oh! Jim,' he said, 'for God's sake, let some one come and read the Bible to me before I die.'

"None of the sailors had a Bible; but at last I found that there was one on board belonging to the cabin-boy. I told him to get his Bible, and bring it into the sick ward, and went back there myself. Presently the boy came with a small Bible in his hand. In the meantime a number of the Kroomen, or native Africans, who were working on board, gathered round the sick man, not to see him die, but, as one of them said—'to see what de good book do for poor massa Richie.'

"I told the boy to read a chapter. He sat down by the sick man, and opening at the third chapter of St. John, he began to read. The poor fellow fixed his eyes on the reader, and listened most earnestly to every word he spoke. Presently the boy came to the beautiful words in the sixteenth verse: 'God so loved the world that he gave his only begotten Son, that whosoever believeth in him should not perish, but have everlasting life!' I watched the face of the dying man as these words were read. I never saw such earnestness and anxiety in any face as were in his. The boy was going on with the next verse, when the sick man exclaimed—'Stop! my boy, stop. Read that verse again, and read it slowly.' The boy repeated the verse, and then was going on again. But he was interrupted a second, and a third time, with the earnest cry, 'Stop, my boy, stop. Read that verse again.' And when he had done so a number of times, the dying man said: 'Don't read any more. That's enough.' And then, as he grew fainter and fainter, we heard him, in a low voice repeating those wonderful words, and making his own remarks on them:—'*Whoso-ever*—that means any body. That means me. Whosoever *believeth*. I do believe this. Well, what then? Whosoever believeth shall *not per-ish*.—No, not perish, but have everlasting life. Not perish—not perish—but have everlasting life.' These were his last words. With these upon his lips, he passed away, and entered into heaven—'one pardoned sinner more,' saved through the precious blood of Christ."

The presence of Jesus which the Tabernacle illustrates is—a pardoning presence.

The next thing that the Tabernacle taught about the presence of Christ with his people was, *that it would be a*—PURIFYING—*presence.*

This was taught by the brazen laver, which was next to the altar of burnt offering, in the Court of the Tabernacle. This laver was kept full of water for the use of the priests and Levites as they were engaged in the service of God. Their hands or feet must not be soiled while they were so engaged. The laver stood near them, and they could go and wash there, when-ever it was necessary. If that brazen laver could have spoken, it would have been repeating, con-stantly the words which God afterwards spoke by the prophet Isaiah, when he said—"*Be ye clean*, that bear the vessels of the Lord." Is. lii: 11. God is a holy God. He dwells in the high and holy place. And if we wish to be his servants now, and to live with him forever hereafter, we must try to be like him in this respect. His command to all his people is—"Be ye holy, for I am holy." Levit. xx: 7. When the king of a country has a reception of the princes, and nobles, and great people of the kingdom, every one who appears before the king is expected to wear a particular kind of dress, which is called the court-dress. No one would be allowed to enter there without such a dress. And there is a court-dress for us to wear if we expect to be admitted to the presence of the King of heaven. This dress is holy dress. "Without holiness," the Apostle Paul tells us—"no man shall see the Lord." Heb. xii: 14.

At one of the ragged-schools in Ireland, a clergyman was talking to the scholars on this very point. In the course of his talk he asked the question—"What is holiness?" A poor Irish boy, in dirty tattered rags, jumped up, and said—"Please yer Riverence, it's to be *clane inside*."

No better answer than this could be given. And one reason why Jesus dwells with his people now, is to make them clean inside. And the laver in the Tabernacle was a good illustration of the way in which he does this. When the hands of one of the priests were soiled, he would go there, and wash, and be made clean. And so when our hearts or thoughts are soiled by sin, Jesus has a laver for us to wash in. The apostle Paul shows how this is done, when he tells us that Jesus "sanctifies or cleanses his people by the *washing of water by the word*." Ephes. v: 26. This means that just as we make use of water to wash our bodies, and cleanse them when soiled, so Jesus makes use of the truths which he teaches in his word to "cleanse the thoughts of our hearts," and to make our souls pure and holy. And thus we see that one thing which the Tabernacle taught us, was that the presence of Jesus with his people was intended to be a cleansing, or purifying presence.

Another thing about the presence of Jesus, taught by the Tabernacle was, *that it was to be an*—ENLIGHTENING—*presence*.

There was no window in the Jewish Tabernacle. The light of the sun, or the moon, or the stars never shone there. The only light ever known within the walls of that sacred building was that which shone from the golden candlestick.   If that candlestick had not been lighted it would have been impossible to see anything connected with the inside of the Tabernacle.   There were the beautiful figures of the angels embroidered on the curtain which formed the ceiling of the holy place.   There was the polished gold on the walls; with the table of shew-bread, and the altar of incense, and the way into the most holy place, through the veil that hung down before it; but darkness, like that of Egypt, would have covered all these things.   No one would ever have been able to see them if the light from that golden candle-stick had not been shining there.   It was only this light which made it possible to see any of these important things.

And this candlestick was a figure or type of Jesus, our Saviour.   He said of himself—"I am the light of the world.   He that followeth me shall not walk in darkness, but shall have the light of life."   John viii: 12.   And all that we know about God, and heaven, and the way to get there, we learn from Jesus.   And when the light which Jesus gives begins to shine upon us, it is not like the light of a lamp, or a candle, or of the sun.   These lights are the same at one time as at another.   But the light that Jesus gives is a steadily increasing light. "It shineth more and more unto the perfect day." Prov. iv: 18.

An aged Christian once said: "I've travelled this road for forty years, and it grows brighter all the way."

When we learn to know Jesus, and walk in the light which his blessed presence gives, we shall be ready to take up the lines of Bonar's sweet hymn, and say:

> " I heard the voice of Jesus say,
>   ' I am this dark world's light;
> Look unto me, thy morn shall rise,
>   And all thy day be bright.'
> I looked to Jesus, and I found
>   In him my star, my sun;
> And in that light of life I'll walk,
>   Till travelling days are done."

Here is the experience of a little blind boy, which shows what a blessed light the presence of Jesus gives.

This boy had an attack of scarlet fever, which left him perfectly blind. One day his minister called to see him. In talking about this affliction, he said:

"Well, my dear boy, this is hard for you, isn't it?"

He did not answer for a moment; then he said, "I don't know that I ought to say *hard*;

God knows best;" but his lips quivered, and a little tear stole down his cheek.

"Yes, my child; you have a kind Saviour who loves you, and feels for you even more than your mother does."

"I know it, sir," said the little boy, "and it comforts me."

"I wish Jesus was here to *cure* Frank," said his little sister.

"Well," said I, "he will open the eyes of little Frank's soul to see what a dear loving Saviour he is. He will show him that a blind heart is worse than blind eyes; and he will help him to see and enjoy heavenly things in all their beauty, and this will make him a thousand times happier than many children who have the use of their bodily eyes."

"Still I can't help wishing he could see," said Lizzie.

"I dare say; but I hope you don't try to make Frank discontented."

"Frank isn't discontented," said Lizzie, earnestly; "he loves God. And love makes its own sunshine; doesn't it, Frank?"

"I don't feel cross about it now," said the poor blind boy meekly. I pray, and think about the sweet hymns I learned in Sabbath school, and I sing, and sing, and then I think that Jesus is with me, and it feels light, and—and—I forget that I'm blind at all;" and a sweet light played over his pale features as he spoke. *That* was the light which the presence of Jesus gives. The Tabernacle taught us that his presence with his people was intended to be an enlightening presence.

The only other thing to speak of now, that the Tabernacle taught, in reference to Christ's presence with his people, was that it will be a— COMFORTING—*presence.*

There was the table of shew-bread. This was a table covered over with gold, and on which twelve fresh loaves of bread were placed every Sabbath day. It was intended to teach the Jews what God teaches us in that sweet promise which says:—"Bread shall be given him, and his water shall be sure." Is. xxxiii: 16. This table of shew-bread pointed to Jesus. He is "the living bread that came down from heaven; if any man eat of this bread he shall live forever." John vi: 51. And we know how bread strengthens, or comforts men's hearts.

And then the golden altar of incense taught the same thing. As the priest burnt the incense on this altar, the perfume rose in clouds of

Jesus in the Wilderness

And he was there in the wilderness forty days, tempted of Satan.
. . . And when he had fasted forty days and forty nights, he was afterward an hungred. And when the tempter came to him, he said, If thou be the Son of God, command that these stones be made bread.   But he answered and said, It is written, Man shall not live by bread alone, but by every word that proceedeth out of the mouth of God.—*St. Mark i: 13; St. Matt. iv: 2–4.*

NOTE BY THE ARTIST

Imagination fails to picture a scene of more terrible desolation and utter solitude than is presented by the ravine which age-long tradition indicates as the spot which witnessed that forty days' conflict between good and evil, the chief crises of which are alone described in the gospel narrative. Some frightful convulsion of nature would seem to have rent asunder the cliffs which tower on either hand, whilst the eye seeks in vain amongst the rocks and sand slanting precipitously to the bottom of the gorge, for a trace of the scant vegetation which is to be found elsewhere, even in the most arid and waterless districts of the Judæan wilderness.

15

15

fragrant smoke that filled the Tabernacle. This fragrance was most pleasing and refreshing. And the meaning of it was, that when we love, and serve Jesus, the prayers that we offer to God and the work that we do for him are just as pleasant to him as the fragrance of this incense is to us. How much comfort there is in this thought!

And then all the things in the Tabernacle, —the brazen altar of burnt-offering, the laver, the candlestick, the table of shew-bread, and the golden altar of incense were intended to lead the thoughts of those who worshiped there to what was on the other side of the veil that hung down in the holy place. There, beyond that veil, was the most holy place. In it was the ark, with the glory of God shining brightly upon it. That place represented heaven. And so, when we see the Tabernacle showing us how Jesus was to be with his people, to pardon them, and to purify them, and to enlighten them, and strengthen them, we see it teaching us how *all* that Jesus does for his people now is to make them ready for heaven. And if this is so, we may well say that the presence of Jesus with his people is a comforting presence.

We have just had an illustration of one point of our subject from a little blind boy. We have another illustration here from an old blind woman.

She lived in North Wales, and was known all through that part of the country as "Blind Mary." Wales is a grand old country. Mountains, and rocks, and lakes, and waterfalls in every variety of form are found there. Mary's cottage was in one of the wildest parts of this country. Great rocks lay scattered around on every side. Ferns and wild flowers peeped out from under them. There was no more charming view in all that country than was to be seen in front of Mary's cottage. One beautiful summer evening she was sitting there, with her large Bible on her knee. She was spelling out its meaning as her fingers went slowly over the raised letters. Just then a traveller who had been climbing the mountain came near. With the usual quickness of the blind, Mary heard his footsteps, and asked him to take a seat. As he did so, she pointed out to him the most interesting views in the landscape before them. He looked at her with surprise, and said: "They told me that *blind* Mary lived up here; but I can hardly believe that you are blind. You seem to see the mountains and lakes as well as I do."

"I used to look at them with so much pleasure when I could see, that I know all about them, although I have been blind for years."

"Doesn't it make you unhappy Mary to think that you can never look at them again?"

The blind woman's eyes filled with tears, as she answered: "Don't ask me that, sir. At first I felt almost angry with God for afflicting me so; but now, I can bless his holy name. I see something better, sir, than rocks and mountains. I see Jesus my Saviour, and the thought that he loves me, makes me happy. Forgive an old woman's boldness, sir. You tell me you have good eyesight, and that you can see yonder lakes, and the blue mountains beyond; but, oh! sir, did you ever see that wonderful sight, Jesus Christ laying down his life for you?"

The traveller looked at blind Mary with great interest, and said:—"Mary, I am afraid I have not thought about these things as I ought; but I promise you that I will do so; I shall never forget my evening's climb up these mountains, and what you have said to me."

"God bless you, sir! But what should I, a poor old blind woman do without my Saviour!

I'm never alone, for he is with me. I'm not afraid to die, either, because he has washed away my sins in his blood; and when I leave these mountains, and lakes, I shall go, I know, to a better country. 'Mine eyes shall see the King in his beauty; they shall behold the land that is very far off.' And I believe I shall meet you there, because I shall ask my Saviour to open your eyes, that you may see yourself first as a sinner, and then see Jesus as your redeemer."

Certainly the presence of Jesus was a comforting presence to poor blind Mary.

And so, we have seen *what the Tabernacle was*, and *what the Tabernacle taught*. It taught how the presence of Christ was to be with his people, as a *pardoning* presence—a *purifying* presence—an *enlightening* presence, and a *comforting* presence. May we all know what it is to have his presence with us, in all these blessed ways!

CHRIST A PRIEST LIKE MELCHIZEDEK

HOW it was foretold of our blessed Saviour that he was to be—"a prophet like Moses," we have seen in the chapter—*"Jesus a Prophet like Moses."* But David gives us another illustration of his character and work, when he tells us that he was to be "a priest forever, after the order of Melchizedek." Ps. cx: 4. This is the next thing for us to consider.

And before we go any further, some one may be ready to ask;—Well, but who was Melchizedek; and what is meant when we are told that Jesus Christ was to be a priest like him? I will try and answer these questions before saying anything else.

The first time that Melchizedek is mentioned in the Bible is in the fourteenth chapter of Genesis. And this mention of him is connected with an interesting incident in the life of Abraham.

There was a great battle fought in his neighborhood when he lived in Hebron. We read about this in the fourteenth chapter of Genesis. We cannot say that this was the first battle ever fought, but it was certainly the first of which we have any knowledge. There was a famous king in those days, who had a long name of five syllables. It was spelled thus—Che-dor-la-o-mer. This man raised a large army and fought with the kings of Sodom and Gomorrah. He beat these kings and gained a great victory over them. He robbed their cities, and took away gold and silver, and valuable things to an immense extent. Besides this he took a great number of prisoners, and carried them away with him as captives. Now it happened that Abraham's nephew, Lot, with his family, was living in Sodom at this time; and they were among the number of those who were taken captives by this famous king. Some one went and told Abraham about it. He was not a soldier. Fighting was not his business. But he was a brave man. As soon as he heard, then, that his nephew and his family had been taken prisoners, he made up his mind to try and rescue them. Abraham was like one of the great Arab Sheiks, who are found in that country at the present day. He had a large number of hired servants connected with his home and the work that was done there. He gathered these together, and armed them the best way he could. They made a small army of over three hundred men. Abraham put himself at the head of them, and marched after the victorious army of the king with a big name. He overtook them before they had reached their homes. They had no idea of being attacked, and felt secure from all danger. No guards or sentinels were appointed to keep watch. They were spending the night in eating and drinking and making merry. In the midst of this merriment Abraham overtakes them. He divides his little army into three companies. Approaching cautiously from different points, at a given signal they raise a great shout, and burst upon that careless host, as the lion leaps upon his prey. Terror seizes upon them. They are scattered in a moment, like a flock of trembling sheep. Abraham is not anxious to shed blood, and does not care to pursue them. But he seizes all the spoils they had gathered, with the prisoners they had taken away, and marches back to his home with his brave little army, and the captives they had recovered.

And it is just here that we first meet with Melchizedek. We read—Gen. xiv: 18-20—that as Abraham was returning, Melchizedek, who was king of a city in Palestine, called Salem, and who was also "priest of the most high God," came out to meet him. He had prepared bread and wine for the refreshment of Abraham and his army, and he blessed Abraham. This is all that is told us about Melchizedek in this part of the Bible. David speaks of him in Ps. cx: 4, and says that Christ was to be "a priest forever after the order of Melchizedek." And here we may well ask the question—What was "the order of Melchizedek?" or what kind of a priest was he? and what does it mean when we are told that our Lord Jesus Christ was to be "a priest like Melchizedek?" The apostle Paul tells us all that we know about this matter. What he says on this point we find written in Heb. vii: 1-3. And the meaning of what he here says is, that in his office as a priest, Melchizedek had no one to go before him, and no one to follow after him. When Aaron, the Jewish high-priest died, his son, Eleazar was made priest in his place. And when Eleazar died, he had his son to succeed him in his priestly office. The eldest son always followed his father in his office as priest. And so there was a succession of priests in the order to which Aaron belonged. But it was different with Melchizedek. He had no one to be priest before him, and no one to be priest after him. There was no succession in the order of his priesthood. And so it was with the blessed Saviour of whom we are writing. In his office as priest there was no one who went before him, and no one who followed after him. In this respect he was to be "a priest forever after the order of Melchizedek." No one was to take his place. No one *could* take it. And it is a very sweet thing to know that whatever Jesus, as our priest, does for us *now*, he will continue to do forever and ever.

And when we think of a priest of God, in his high and holy office, there are four things he is appointed to do for his people, and in each of these things the Jewish priest was a type or figure of Christ.

The first thing that a priest had to do was, to— TEACH.

We read in Malachi ii: 7, these words,—"The priest's lips should keep knowledge, and they should seek the law at his mouth; for he is the messenger of the Lord of hosts." Here we have

God's own account of the first thing that he
wished his priests to do. And when we are told
that "the priest's lips should *keep* knowledge,"
the meaning is, *not* that he was to keep knowledge *from* the people, but that he was to keep
it *for* them.

When our Saviour was on earth, he said that
the priests and the Pharisees were keeping
knowledge from the people. Luke xi: 52. And
other priests since then have done the same
thing. But this is not what God intended. His
wish was that the priests whom he appointed
should be as his messengers, always ready to
show people the right way in which to worship
and serve God, when they desired to know it.

And this is what Jesus came into our world
to do. He is the great teacher. There is none
who can teach like him. All the knowledge
that we have of God in this world comes from
him. This is what he taught us himself, when
he said:—"No man knoweth the Father save
the Son, and he to whom the Son will reveal
him." Matt. xi: 27. "No man hath seen God
at any time, the only begotten Son, who is in
the bosom of the Father, he hath declared him."
John i: 18. And the things that Jesus taught
when on earth, he said, were only the things

which he had seen with his Father, and which the Father sent him into the world to tell us. He was teaching all the time he was on earth. And he did not stop teaching when he went back to heaven. By his word, by his spirit, by his ministers, by his people, and in other ways he is teaching all the time. Everything that we know about God, or heaven, or the way to get there, we owe to Jesus.

And sometimes he teaches in ways that are very wonderful. Here is an illustration of the marvellous power of Jesus to teach even when the case seemed most hopeless. We may call it—*The Robber Taught;* or, *The Power of the Bible.*"

This incident occurred many years ago in the heart of the Black Forest in Germany. It was at the dead of night. The place was lighted by torches, which cast a ghastly glare through the surrounding gloom. Savage looking men, fully armed, were sitting round in a circle. One of their number was holding up something in his hand. These men were robbers. That evening they had robbed a stage-coach. According to their custom they were now engaged in selling by auction, among themselves, the articles that had been stolen. Travelling bags, different articles of clothing, and various other things had been disposed of in this way. Last of all a New Testament was held up. The man who acted as auctioneer introduced this "article" with some wicked remark which threw the company into a roar of laughter. One of the company suggested as a joke that the auctioneer should open the book and read a chapter, as he said, "for their edification." This motion was seconded, and carried unanimously. Opening the book at random, he began to read with an air of mock solemnity. As he went on reading, laughs and jokes were heard all round.

While this was going on, one man in the company, the oldest member of the gang, and who had been their ringleader in all that was evil, became silent. He sat with his hands clasped on his knees, lost in deep thought. It happened that the passage the auctioneer had just read was the very one he had heard read thirty years before, at family prayer in his father's house, on the morning of the day when he left that home for the last time. In a moment all that scene came back to his memory. He thought of his father and mother, and brothers and sisters, and all that had made that home so sweet and happy to him then. Since leaving home he had never opened a Bible, never offered a prayer, and never had a thought of God, or of eternity.   But now, in a moment, his soul seemed to wake from that long sleep of thirty years.   He thought of God; he thought of his wicked life, and was filled with sorrow, and shame, and fear.   He was so occupied with these thoughts and feelings, that he took no notice of what was going on around him till one of his comrades slapped him rudely on the shoulder, and said,—"Now, old dreamer, what will you give for that book? you need it most of all, for you have been the biggest sinner among us."

"That's true," said the startled robber.   "Give me that book, I'll pay the full price for it."

The next day the robbers scattered, and went into the neighboring towns and villages to sell what they had got by robbing.   The man with the Testament also went away.   But he did not wish to sell any thing.   He sought a quiet, lonely place.   There he remained for several days, reading that wonderful book of God, shedding bitter tears over his sins, and earnestly praying for God's pardoning grace.   God heard his prayer.   He found pardon and peace in believing, and became a new man.

After awhile he went into one of the nearest towns to see a minister of the gospel. There he heard that the gang of robbers to which he had belonged had all been taken prisoners. He told the minister, whom he went to see, all about his previous life, and the change he had experienced. Then he gave himself up to the officers of justice. The rest of the gang were all put to death. But his free confession and evident repentance saved his life. He was put in prison, indeed; but, as he continued to behave like a truly penitent man, he was soon pardoned and released, and taken into the employment of one of the princes in that neighborhood, and he proved a blessing to those about him all his days.

This was wonderful teaching indeed! And the first thing that Jesus does as our priest, is to —*teach*.

The second thing that a priest had to do, was to—ATONE.

And here you may be ready to ask what does it mean to atone? or to make an atonement? Let us try to get a clear idea of this matter. Now suppose, that in some way, you should greatly offend a person who had been your best friend. The thought of it distresses you. What

Satan's Failure

Again, the devil taketh him up into an exceeding high mountain, and sheweth him all the kingdoms of the world, and the glory of them. And saith unto him, All these things will I give thee, if thou wilt fall down and worship me.   Then saith Jesus unto him, Get thee hence, Satan: for it is written, Thou shalt worship the Lord thy God, and him only shalt thou serve.   Then the devil leaveth him, and, behold, angels came and ministered unto him.—*St. Matt. iv: 8–11.*

NOTE BY THE ARTIST

Whether a mental or an optical vision of the kingdoms of the world is referred to in the text, it is clearly stated that the last temptation took place upon an "exceeding high mountain"; and as mountains of exceptional altitude are invariably capped with snow, a snow-peak, touched with earliest sunrise, is therefore selected as the scene of Satan's final and greatest effort of temptation, and of its failure.

16

shall I do, you ask yourself, to remove the anger of my friend and have him reconciled to me again? You hear that your friend is very anxious to get a jewel of a particular kind. It is very costly. You know where such a jewel can be had. You have to part with all you have in the world to get it. But you do this gladly. You get the jewel. You send it to your friend, telling him, at the same time how sorry you are for having offended him, and asking him to forgive you. He accepts your gift. His anger is turned away and he is reconciled to you again. Now, in getting that jewel, and giving it to your friend, you would be making an atonement for what you had done to offend him.

This illustrates what we are now speaking of. God is our best friend. We have offended him by our sins. He never could be reconciled to us unless our sins were put away. But we had no power to do this. All the angels in heaven never could have done it for us. Jesus was the only one who was able to do it. And he was willing to do it. And the apostle Paul shows us the way in which he did this, when he tells us that Christ—"came *to put away sin, by the sacrifice of himself.*" Heb. ix: 26. And that is what is meant when we are told that he "made peace through the blood of his cross." Col. i: 20. By his sufferings in the garden of Gethsemane, and by his death upon the cross he atoned for our sins, or put them away. Thus it became possible that our quarrel with God should be made up; and that there should be, as the angels said in their song over the birth of Christ, "peace on earth, and good will towards men."

But Jesus, our priest, did not come into the world to make atonement for our sins till four thousand years had passed away. Yet, people needed pardon and peace during all those years, as much as we do now. And how were they to know the way in which these great blessings were to be obtained? God appointed sacrifices to be offered in order to help the people to understand this. The chief duty of the Jewish priest, was to stand by the brazen altar, and offer there a lamb for a sacrifice, every morning and every evening. The blood of those animals could not atone for sin, or put it away. But they pointed to Jesus who was coming to do this. All the sacrifices that we read about in the Old Testament did this. There was Abel's sacrifice, the first that we read of.

This pointed to Jesus. And there was Abraham, binding his son Isaac, laying him on the altar, and taking the knife to slay him. Abraham was pointing to Jesus when he did this.

And when the pious Jew brought his lamb to the altar to be sacrificed for him, as the blood of that lamb was shed, and his life taken away God was leading the man who offered that sacrifice, to look away from the service in which he was engaged, and to "behold," Jesus, "the lamb of God who taketh away the sins of the world." John i: 29. And this is what is meant when Jesus is spoken of as "the Lamb slain from the foundation of the world." Rev. xiii: 8. Every lamb slain by the Jewish priests was a type or figure of Christ, and so, it may be said that he was slain in them.

All that Jesus did, and suffered, when he was on earth, he did and suffered for you, and me. And when we believe on him, God looks upon us as he would do if we ourselves had done and suffered all that Jesus did and suffered for us.

"He died for me."—During the late war between France and Germany, an incident occurred which well illustrates this part of our subject. A young man was drafted into the army. He was the only son of his mother. She was a widow, and dependent on him for her support. They were both in great distress about it. A friend of this young man saw his distress. He said to him, "Louis, you stay at home, and take care of your mother. There's no one depending on me. Let me be your substitute, and go in your place."

Louis objected for awhile, but finally yielded. His generous friend went to the war in his place. In the first battle that was fought he was killed. The friend whose place he had taken, mourned sincerely over his death.

But the war went on. The drafting was continued. By some mistake Louis was counted in again, and ordered to join the army. He went to the recruiting office, and asked if it was true that his name was on the list of drafted men.

"It is," replied the officer.

"But dead men cannot serve," said he, "and I am a dead man."

The officer looked at him with surprise, and said: "Well, my friend, I never saw a dead man speak and act as you are doing. You seem lively enough, and are just the sort of man we want. Pray tell me what you mean by saying you are a dead man."

"Well, sir," said Louis, "I was drafted before, and was preparing to go. But a generous friend offered himself as my substitute. He went for me. He fought for me. He laid down his life on the field of battle. And as he stood in my place, and died in my stead, it is as if I no longer lived. The life that I now live was purchased by the life of my friend. *He died for me! he died for me!* and I must go free."

"That's all right," said the officer, "you are free."

And so what Jesus did and suffered while he was on earth, he did and suffered for you, and me, if we believe in him. He made atonement for our sins. They are all "blotted out," or "put away." God is reconciled to us. "Being justified by faith, we have peace with God, through our Lord Jesus Christ." Rom. v: 1.

The second thing that Jesus does as our priest, is to atone.

The third thing that a priest had to do for the people, was to—INTERCEDE—for them.

This word intercede is made up of two Latin words, the meaning of which is to *walk between.* For instance, if you see two persons quarrelling, and step in between them to separate them, then you are interceding, or walking

between them. This is the first meaning of
the word.

But there is another sense in which this word
is used. When we pray for other persons, and
ask God to guard them from danger, or to
bestow his blessing upon them, then we are
said to be *interceding* for them. In this sense,
to intercede for a person, is to pray for him.
We have an interesting illustration of this in the
eighteenth chapter of Genesis.

Here we read that God appeared before Abraham, in the form of a man, or an angel. He
tells him that he is going to destroy the cities
of Sodom and Gomorrah, for their great wickedness. As soon as Abraham hears this, he feels
anxious about his nephew, Lot, who is living
there with his family. Immediately, Abraham
begins to pray for those wicked cities, which
were in such danger of being destroyed. He
asks God if he will not spare them, in case he
should find fifty good or righteous people living
there. He said he would. But not satisfied
with that, Abraham wants to make the prospect
of their safety greater still. With very great
reverence, he asks God if he will spare those
cities in case there are forty righteous people in
them. The answer is—yes. But suppose there

are but thirty? I will spare them for the sake
of thirty. Suppose there are only twenty? I
will spare them for the sake of twenty. Suppose
there are but ten? I will not destroy them, if
there are even ten good people there. And
then Abraham stopped praying. He thought
it was safe to do this. He felt sure there would
be at least ten good people found there. But
he was mistaken. Lot was the only good man
there; and he was none too good, or else he
would not have been willing to stay in that
horribly wicked place, when he was not obliged
to do so.

Now, when Abraham was offering these
prayers for Sodom and Gomorrah, he was *interceding* for them. He was walking between God
and them, and trying to do them good.

And this was one important part of the duty
which the Jewish priest had to perform for the
people. It was especially the duty of the high-
priest. Every year, on what was called—"the
great day of atonement," the high-priest would
put on his beautiful garments, of blue, and
scarlet, and purple. And then he would put
on the breast-plate. This was a square plate
about eight inches wide, and eight deep. The
front of it was covered with gold. In this gold

were set twelve beautiful jewels, or precious
stones. On these were engraved the names of
the twelve tribes of Israel, one on each stone.
There were ribbons of blue, at the lower corners
of this plate, and cords of gold at the upper
corners. By these it was fastened to the shoulders of the high-priest. And then, bearing the
names of all the tribes upon his bosom, he went
into the most holy place, to stand before God,
and intercede, or pray for the people. And as
he did this, he was illustrating in a beautiful
way, what Jesus, our great high-priest, is doing
for us.

In the seventeenth chapter of the Gospel of
St. John, we have an example of Jesus praying
for his people. That whole chapter is filled
with the prayer which he offered in the night
in which he was betrayed. It is the most
wonderful prayer that was ever uttered. Jesus
begins with praying for himself. Then he prays
for his apostles. After this, in verse twenty, he
says: "Neither pray I for these alone, but for
them also which shall believe on me through
their word." This takes you and me in, if we
believe in Jesus. How sweet it is to think that
Jesus really stands before the throne of God in
heaven, and prays for each one of us! Yet this

is what the apostle Paul means, when he says, in speaking of Jesus, that—"*he ever liveth to make intercession for us.*" Heb. vii: 25. And when our prayers are answered, this is what brings the answer to us. Jesus has prayed for us. God has heard his prayers. The proof of this we have in the answers that come down in blessings upon us.

"I feel it pull." A little boy was flying his kite. It had gone up until it was out of sight. But there he stood holding on to the string which was fastened to it. A gentleman in passing said to him, "What are you holding on to that string for, my boy?"

"Because there is a kite at the other end of it."

"I don't see any kite," said the gentleman.

"Ah! but I know it's there," was the reply, "for *I feel it pull.*"

And so it is with what we are now speaking of. We cannot look through an open door into heaven, as the apostle John did. Rev. iv: 1. We cannot with our bodily eyes see Jesus interceding, or praying for us. But *we know he is there.* And every prayer answered is a proof of this. And then, like the boy just spoken of, though we cannot see the kite, we know it is there because we feel it pull.

"What stopped that train?" Not long ago an engineer brought his train to a stand at a little village in Massachusetts. There it waited five minutes for lunch. A lady came along the platform to the engineer. She said to him:

"My friend, the conductor tells me that the train at the junction in P., leaves fifteen minutes before we arrive there. It is Saturday night, and that is the last train. I have a very sick child in the car, and am extremely anxious to catch that train. I have no money to pay for going to a hotel, nor to hire a carriage to take me home from that point. What shall I do?"

"Well," said the engineer, "I wish I could tell you."

"Wouldn't it be possible for you to hurry up a little?" asked the tearful and anxious mother.

"No, madam, I have the time-table and the rules say I must run by it."

She turned away sorrowfully, leaving the bronzed face of the engineer wet with tears. Presently she returned, and said to the engineer, "Are you a Christian, sir?"

"I trust I am," was the reply.

"Well, then, won't you pray with me that the Lord may, in some way, delay the train at the junction?"

"Why, yes, I'll pray with you, but I haven't much faith."

Just then the conductor cried—"All aboard." The poor woman hurried back to her sick child, and away went the train.

"Somehow," said the engineer, "every thing seemed to work to a charm. As I prayed for the anxious mother, I *couldn't help letting my engine go a little faster.* We were not delayed a moment at any of the stopping places. When the last stopping place was passed, and we were over the hill, as I knew the road was all clear and there was no danger, I put on more steam. We went flying through the air like an arrow; and presently we dashed up to the junction six minutes ahead of time.

To my great surprise, there stood the other train and the conductor with his lantern on his arm. "Well," said he; "here I am nine minutes behind time. I never did such a thing before. I can't, for the life of me, tell what I have been waiting for. But somehow or other it seemed as if I couldn't go till this train came in."

The conductor of that train didn't know what he was waiting for. But the engineer of the other train knew. And that poor, grateful mother knew, as she was enabled, with her sick child, to reach home in comfort that night. She could say with the boy and his kite, "*I feel it pull.*" She knew who was in heaven praying for her.

The third thing that the priest did for the people, was to intercede for them. And this is what Jesus, our "Priest like Melchizedek," does for us.

*But there was one other thing which the Jewish priests were required to do for their people, and that was, to—*BLESS—*them.*

We have seen before (Gen. xiv: 18) how Melchizedek met Abraham returning from his victory, and blessed him. And Jewish priests were required to give the blessing, or, as we say, "pronounce the benediction," at the close of their religious meetings, as the ministers of the gospel do now. And this was especially done at the close of the solemn service held among the Jews every year, on what was called—"the great day of atonement." Then the high-priest, dressed in his beautiful robes, came out of the Tabernacle, where he had been sprinkling the blood of the sacrifice and offering prayer for the people. He stood in the midst of them and lifted up his hands and blessed them. We know what the words were which the priests used on these occasions. We find them in Numbers, sixth chapter, twenty-fourth to twenty-sixth verses. They are these:

"The Lord bless thee, and keep thee; the Lord make his face shine upon thee, and be gracious unto thee; the Lord lift up his countenance upon thee, and give thee peace."

These words are very beautiful. But then, the Jewish priests could only use them as a kind of prayer. They could ask God to give these blessings to the people; and they could tell the people how to seek these blessings. But they had no power to give the people these blessings.

And here we see the great difference between all other priests and Jesus, our heavenly priest. He not only speaks the words of blessing, but he really gives the blessings those words represent. This was what he meant when he said to his disciples, "Peace I leave with you; my peace I give unto you; not as the world giveth, give I unto you." John xiv: 27. The world or the people in the world can only wish, or pray, that we may have peace. But Jesus can *give* peace. Yes, and not only peace, but pardon, and hope, and joy, and grace, and every blessing that we

need Jesus is able to give.   He came to bless the
world.   He *did* bless it while he was in it.   He
"went about doing good."   He was scattering
blessings wherever he went.   And he is doing
the same still.   He loves to bless.   And the
store of blessings he has to draw upon is so large
and full that it never can fail.

Look at yonder sun.   For thousands of years
it has been shining away all the time.   And
yet the sun has as much light to give to-day, as
it had in the day when God first made it.   Or,
look at yonder ocean.   It has been giving up its
water to supply the springs and fountains of the
earth ever since it was made.   And yet there is
as much water in the ocean to-day as there was
thousands of years ago.   And so it is with Jesus.
For thousands of years he has been giving away
blessings continually.   And yet he has as many
to give to-day as though he had never given
one before.   He *came* to bless the world.   He
has blessed it, and he *is* blessing it still.   He is
blessing nations, and families, and individuals,
in such a way as nothing else can bless them.
When we learn to know him, and love him, and
trust him, the thought of what he has done for
us already, and what he is going to do for us
by and by, is enough to make us happy at all

John Points to Jesus

Again the next day after John stood, and two of his disciples. And looking upon Jesus as he walked, he saith, Behold the Lamb of God! And the two disciples heard him speak, and they followed Jesus. Then Jesus turned, and saw them following, and saith unto them, What seek ye? They said unto him, Rabbi, (which is to say, being interpreted, Master,) where dwellest thou? He saith unto them, Come and see. They came and saw where he dwelt, and abode with him that day: for it was about the tenth hour. One of the two which heard John *speak*, and followed him, was Andrew, Simon Peter's brother. He first findeth his own brother Simon, and saith unto him, We have found the Messias, which is, being interpreted, the Christ. And he brought him to Jesus. And when Jesus beheld him, he said, Thou art Simon the son of Jona: thou shalt be called Cephas, which is by interpretation, A stone.— *St. John i: 35–42.*

NOTE BY THE ARTIST

Jesus lodging on the banks of the Jordan, at which place his earliest disciples were attracted by his words and teaching, was probably one of those black goat-hair tents in common use among the wandering inhabitants of the "Ghor," or Lower Jordan Valley.

17

17

times, and under all circumstances. It is, as Jesus said, like "a well of water in our hearts, springing up into everlasting life." John iv: 14. Here is an incident which shows how true it is that simple trust in Jesus will prove a blessing under all the trials of life.

"John White's Hymn." A minister of the gospel was travelling through the wilds of Nebraska. Late one evening he lost his way. In the midst of a pelting storm he sought shelter in the cabin of a lonely Irish settler. He was warmly welcomed, and they spent a pleasant evening talking together. At the close of the evening his Irish friend said to him, "Now, sir, will you please sing something before we go to rest? Can you sing John White's hymn?"

"John White's hymn? No, I never heard of that. What is it?"

"It's this, sir:

> "'Away with our sorrow and fear,
> We soon shall reach our home;
> The city of saints shall appear,
> The day of eternity come.'

"O, yes! I've sung that good old hymn many a time. But why do you call it John White's hymn?"

"I'll tell you, sir. When we were young people in old Ireland—my wife and I—we attended a meeting, where we learned to love Jesus. The minister was a young man named John White. He spent all his time among the people, telling them of the love of Jesus, and trying to persuade them to love and serve him. He was often persecuted on account of his religion, but he never answered those who troubled him, except by singing some of the verses of this blessed hymn. My wife and I learned to sing it together, and it has been the greatest comfort to us. We have had many sorrows to bear, but when we sang this sweet hymn, and thought of the dear, loving Saviour, it always lightened our burdens, and made us happy.

"A few years after we settled here, our little boy, our only child, lay dying. That was a heavy blow. The mother stood on one side of the cradle, and I on the other. We watched the death-drops gather on that patient little face. Then my wife looked up to me and said, 'O, Pat, sing John White's hymn.' So, softly, and with a choking voice, I sang:

> "'Away with our sorrow and fear,
>   We soon shall reach our home.'

"And we closed the little eyes, that were never more to look into ours, until that glad 'day of eternity come.'

"A few months after this, sir, came the greatest trial of my life. My dear wife, who had always been such a comfort to me, was taken very ill. The doctor said she could not live. As I sat by her bedside, overwhelmed with sorrow, she put her arm around my neck, and drawing my face down close to hers, she gently whispered, 'Good bye, Pat, dear. I'm going home. Sing John White's hymn for me, once more before I go. So, with her cold hand clasped in mine, I tried to sing:

> "'Away with our sorrow and fear,
> We soon shall reach our home.'

"And the Lord took away my sorrow and fear. My dear patient wife was quite happy till she fell asleep in Jesus."

Then the Irish settler wiped away the tears from his eyes, and while the storm was howling without, he and the minister, as they sat by the blazing fire sang once more John White's hymn:

> "Away with our sorrow and fear,
> We soon shall reach our home;
> The city of saints shall appear,
> The day of eternity come."

Surely Jesus did bless that poor Irish settler and his wife in all their troubles! And when we remember that what the Jewish priest had to do, was to *teach*—to *atone*—to *intercede* for, and to *bless* the people, we see how truly it might be said of Jesus, that he was to—"be a priest forever, after the order of Melchizedek."

CHRIST THE KING LIKE DAVID AND SOLOMON

WE have spoken before of Christ, as "a Prophet like Moses," and "a Priest like Melchizedek." We come now to speak of him as a king. There are many passages in the Old Testament that speak of him as a king. We need only refer to one of these. In Jer. xxiii: 5, we find it written,—"Behold the days come, saith the Lord, that I will raise unto David a righteous Branch, and a King shall reign and prosper, and shall execute judgment and justice in the earth." It is perfectly clear that Jesus, our blessed Saviour is the one here spoken of, for, in the very next verse, the prophet goes on to say, "In his days Judah shall be saved, and Israel shall dwell safely; and this is his name whereby he shall be called, THE LORD OUR RIGHT-EOUSNESS." Jesus is the only one to whom this name belongs.

227

And when we come to look at the New Testament, we find him spoken of in the same way. He was to be a king.   When the angel Gabriel was sent from God, to the city of Nazareth, to tell of the birth of Jesus, to Mary, his mother, he said to her:—"Thou shalt bring forth a son, and shalt call his name JESUS. He shall be great, and shall be called the Son of the Highest, and the Lord God shall give unto him the throne of his father David; and he shall reign over the house of Jacob; and of his kingdom there shall be no end.

When Jesus was born in Bethlehem, and the wise men came from the East to Jerusalem seeking for him, their inquiry was—"Where is he that is born *King of the Jews?* for we have seen his star in the East, and have come to worship him."   Matt. ii: 1, 2.   And when he hung upon the cross, dying in agony and blood, the title which Pontius Pilate, the Roman Governor fastened to his cross, was:

"THIS IS JESUS THE KING OF THE JEWS."

When Jesus was foretold as a prophet, it was said distinctly what sort of a prophet he was to be. And when he was foretold as a priest, it is again distinctly said what sort of a priest he was

to be.   But when he was foretold as a king, it
was not said, in so many words, that he was to
be a king like David, or Solomon. We are only
told that he was to be the son of David, and he
was to occupy the throne of David.   But when
we are told of the Old Testament history, that
"whatsoever things were written aforetime"
therein "were written for our learning,"—Rom.
xv: 4,—we are authorized to look for illustrations of his character and work as our king, in
the history given us of the principal kings mentioned in the scriptures.

When Jesus is revealed to us as our *prophet*,
we are taught to look for illustrations of what
sort of a prophet he was to be in the character
of Moses, the greatest of the Old Testament
prophets. When he is revealed to us as our
priest, we are taught to look for illustrations of
what he was to do for us as a priest in the life
and character of Melchizedek, who was in some
respects the most remarkable priest of whom
we read in the Old Testament.   And when we
find him spoken of as our *king*, and we wish to
know what sort of a king he was to be, it is
altogether right and proper that we should try
and find our illustrations in the lives and histories of the best and greatest kings, of whose

characters we read in the Old Testament. Of these, David and Solomon were the chief. And then, if the question is asked—What sort of a king was Jesus to be? The answer to that question will take this shape; he was to be a king like David and Solomon. And so the subject before us now, may be stated in this way:

"JESUS A KING LIKE DAVID AND SOLOMON."

We find three illustrations of the kingly character of Christ in David's life, and two in the life of Solomon. And taking these together we have *five* things that will help us in answering the question,—*What sort of a king was Jesus our Saviour to be?*

In the first place then we are taught that he was to be a—CHOSEN—*king.*

Some men have been kings because they wanted to be kings. They made up their minds that they *would* be kings, without any care about the cost, or the consequence. They raised armies, and fought to be kings. They killed all who opposed them, and, as we say, in a figurative sense, they waded through rivers of blood to the throne on which they sat. But we all know very well that this was not the case with David. He did not want to be a king.

I suppose that when he was keeping his father's flocks in the fields of Bethlehem, he had no more idea of being king than you or I have to-day. He did not make himself king; but he was chosen of God to be the king of Israel.

When Saul, the first king of Israel, refused to obey God, he lost his kingdom by his disobedience. God said he would take away the kingdom from him, and give it to another person. And then we know how he sent Samuel, the prophet, to the city of Bethlehem, and to the house of Jesse, to anoint as king, in the place of Saul, one of Jesse's sons, whom he had chosen. God did not mention by name to Samuel which one of the sons of Jesse it was that he had chosen to be king. He gave him to understand that he would let him know this when he got there. I have always thought that it must have been a very interesting scene which took place in the house of Jesse, when Samuel arrived there. Of course, he told Jesse, in confidence, what he had come for. We may imagine Jesse and his family all assembled in the court-yard. You know that in those eastern countries houses are built in the shape of a hollow-square. In the centre is a garden, and if the family are well off, they have a fountain playing in the midst of the garden. Jesse was a rich man. He had, no doubt, a beautiful garden with a fountain in it. He had a large family of eight sons. His two oldest boys were soldiers in Saul's army. They were at home now. Well, the father and mother and the seven elder sons all meet in the garden, to see which of the sons of Jesse God had chosen to be king. I think it was hard on little David that they did not let him come home on such an occasion. They might have let one of the servants go and mind the sheep for an hour or two, till Samuel was gone. But they did not. It must have been a solemn meeting. We should begin such a meeting with reading a portion of scripture and prayer. Samuel began it with offering a sacrifice. No doubt there was a family altar in one part of the garden. When this service was over, Samuel told Jesse to call up his eldest son. Jesse called him. His name was Eliab. He stepped out, and stood before Samuel. He was a fine, tall, soldierly-looking man. Samuel was pleased with his appearance. He said to himself,—"This must be the one. What a handsome looking king he'll make. I'll anoint him."

But God said to him,—"This is not the one I have chosen." "Pass on, young man," said

Samuel. "Call the next." Abinadab steps forward. "This is not the one." "Call the next." Then comes Shammah. "This is not the one." And so, one after another, the seven elder sons of Jesse are called, but none of them is chosen.

"Are these all your sons?" asks Samuel. "No," says Jesse. "There is one more, but he is only a lad, and is minding the sheep." "Send for him," says Samuel. He is sent for. Presently in comes the shepherd boy, with his ruddy face, and his staff in his hand. He was, says the Bible, "of a beautiful countenance, and goodly to look to." God whispers to Samuel,—"Arise, anoint him; for this is he. And he anointed him in the midst of his brethren." I. Sam. xvi: 12, 13.

Thus David was chosen by God to be king. And Jesus was like David in this respect. God says of him,—"I have laid help on one that is mighty; I have exalted one *chosen* out of the people." Ps. lxxxix: 19. In another place when speaking of Christ, he calls him "my servant— my *chosen*, in whom my soul delighteth." Is. xlii: 1; xliii: 10. But there is a difference between this word chosen as applied to David and to Christ.

When David was chosen, there were many other persons among the Israelites who would have made good kings. No doubt any one of David's brothers would have done very well for the king. And there was Jonathan, Saul's eldest son; he would have made a splendid king. Yet God chose David in preference to all the rest.

But it was different with Jesus when he was chosen to be our king. There was none who could have been king in his place. Among all the men in the world there was none. Among all the angels in heaven there was none. In all the other worlds that God has made there was none. When we are told that God hath *chosen* Christ to be our king, the meaning is that he hath chosen the plan of saving and blessing the people through the sufferings and death of his Son, Jesus Christ, in preference to any other plan. And so the first thing in which Jesus is a king like David is that he is—a *chosen* king.

In the second place when told that Jesus is a king like David, we are taught that he was to be a—PREPARED—*king.*

Whatever business we expect to engage in as our life-work, it is necessary that we should make some preparation for it. If a boy determines to be a carpenter, or a mason, or a printer, or a merchant, he must make up his mind to learn that trade or business. Suppose you know a boy named John Smith. He gets through with going to school at the close of December, in one year, and in the first week of January, in the very next year, he has his sign painted and hung out over his door—JOHN SMITH, CARPENTER. He sets up to be a carpenter before he has learned the trade. Would he succeed as a carpenter? No. If you wanted a house built, would you trust *that* John Smith to build it for you? Never. Before setting up to be a carpenter, John Smith ought to spend several years working with some good carpenter, as an apprentice, in order that he might learn the trade. And it is the same with a lawyer, or doctor, or minister, or any other business. No matter how much learning we may have about other things, there must be a special preparation for the particular trade or business that we expect to engage in.

Look at Moses as an illustration. God raised him up to be the ruler, and law-giver, and as it were the king of Israel. Moses was educated in Egypt, as "the son of Pharaoh's daughter." He graduated in their best college. The Egyptians were the most learned people in the world at that time; and Moses had learned all that they could teach him. And yet, when he was forty years old, with all his learning he was not prepared for the work he had to do. A special preparation was necessary to fit him for this work. And so God sent him into the wilderness. There, as a shepherd, he spent forty years more in quiet meditation and prayer, learning to know himself, and to govern his own heart. And *this* was the way in which God prepared him to be the governor and leader of his people.

And here we have David as another illustration. God first *chose* him to be king, and then *prepared* him to be king. David spent his boyhood as a shepherd. This was very useful work for a boy, but minding sheep would not prepare him to be a king. So David had to serve an apprenticeship, and so learn the business of being a king. He enlisted in Saul's army, and became a soldier. In a little while, Saul became jealous of him. Then he got angry with him, and tried to kill him. David had to leave his home, and his family, and go wandering about for seven or eight years in the wilderness, on the mountains, and in dens and caves of the earth, while Saul was pursuing and persecuting him all over the land. It is

"Follow Me"

The day following Jesus would go forth into Galilee, and findeth Philip, and saith unto him, Follow me. Now Philip was of Bethsaida, the city of Andrew and Peter. Philip findeth Nathanael, and saith unto him, We have found him, of whom Moses in the law, and the prophets, did write, Jesus of Nazareth, the son of Joseph.—*St. John i: 43–45.*

NOTE BY THE ARTIST

The scene depicted is familiar to pilgrims, being that kown as the Wady Harâmûyeh, a beautiful valley through which runs the road from Jerusalem to Shechem and Galilee. Jesus and his disciples journeying from the Jordan, would probably join this road at Bethel, which lies a few miles to the south.

18

18

surprising how many narrow and hair-breadth escapes David had during those trying years. Almost every day brought some new danger to him. On two occasions Saul pursued him so closely that, without knowing it, he slept in different parts of the same great cave where David and his men were hid. He could easily have killed Saul then if he had wished to do so. But this was not his desire. Yet on each of these occasions, at the still hour of midnight, David came cautiously up to the place where Saul lay sleeping. His men wanted to kill him, but David would not let them. At one time he took away the spear of Saul from his bolster; and at another, he cut off the hem of his robe, that the king might know how near David had been to him without hurting him. And the lessons that God was teaching David all this time were lessons of patience, and lessons of trust that he was to practise towards God; and lessons of tenderness and sympathy that he was to practise towards his people. He could not have been a good king unless he had learned these lessons well. And as we read about this part of David's life, and think of the painful trials through which he had to pass, we can understand the meaning of it. We see that this was the way in which God was educating him for the high and honorable office he was afterwards to fill. And when, at last, he came to be king over the nation of Israel, he was a *prepared* king.

And David was a figure of Christ in this respect. In a somewhat similar way, Jesus, our Great Saviour, was *prepared* for his office as king. We might think, indeed, that Jesus, as the Son of God, was so strong, so wise, so kind, so loving, as not to need any preparation to fit him for the great office he holds as our king and Saviour. But it is of no consequence what *we think* about such a matter as this. The only thing of any importance is to find out what *God says*. And God tells us that this preparation was needed. It was necessary for Jesus, when he became our king to know, by his own personal experience what temptation, and sorrow, and trouble are.

And there are two passages in the New Testament which teach us what the truth is on this point. In one of these, when the apostle Paul is speaking of Jesus, he says:—*Though he was a son, yet learned he obedience by the things that he suffered.*" Heb. v: 8. We spoke a little while ago of Jesus as our priest. And one of the things he was to do as our priest, was to *teach*. And one of the most important things that Jesus had to teach us, was—*obedience*—how to obey God. And the way in which Jesus teaches us this lesson is by his example. *"He left us an example that we should follow his steps."* I. Rev. ii: 21. He learned obedience himself, that he might be able to teach us this most important lesson.

And the same apostle tells us again, when speaking of Jesus as "the captain of our salvation," that he "was made *perfect through sufferings."* Heb. ii: 10. And when we are told here that Jesus was "made perfect," it does not mean that he was ever imperfect as we are, on account of our sins. Jesus "knew no sin." Not the least shadow of sin ever belonged to him. The sufferings of Jesus made him "perfect" by preparing him to know in his own experience what it is to bear temptations, and sorrows, and trials. And in this way, as our friend and Saviour, he was *prepared* to be our king, loving us, and sympathizing with us when we are bearing sufferings of any kind.

*In the third place, when told that Jesus was to be a king like David, we are taught that he was to be—*A victorious—*king.*

When David was only a boy, he was victorious over his earliest enemies, the lion and the bear that stole away the lambs from his flock. He went after them, without fear. He slew them, and saved his lambs from their devouring jaws. And it was the same when he went to the army, to visit his brothers who were soldiers. There he saw that great giant, Goliath, of Gath, come out from the camp. This proud Philistine shook his fist at the army of Israel, and dared any one to come out and fight him. The bravest soldiers in Saul's army trembled at the sound of his voice. They were all afraid to go. But David was not afraid. He offered to go out and fight the Philistine. His offer was accepted. He went without a sword, or a shield, or a spear. To the boasting Philistine he said:— "Thou comest to me with a sword, and with a spear, and with a shield; but I come to thee in the name of the Lord of hosts, the God of the armies of Israel, whom thou hast defied." I. Samuel xvii: 45. He had nothing with him but his simple sling and a few smooth pebble-stones, taken out of the brook. He fought the giant with his sling alone. He sent one of those stones whizzing through the air. It smote him in the forehead, and brought him headlong to the ground. Then David drew the giant's sword, and smote him, and slew him with it, and took off his head.

And then, in the many battles that he afterwards fought, he was always victorious. He never lost a battle.

And Jesus was like David in this respect. In all that he has undertaken to do, he has proved himself victorious. When his enemies took him prisoner, and nailed him to the cross, they thought they had conquered him for ever. But how greatly they were mistaken! Just then and there he conquered them. The greatest victory Jesus ever gained, was gained as he hung bleeding and dying on the cross. Death and the grave were our great enemies. But while nailed to the tree on Calvary, in the words of the prophet Hosea, Jesus seemed to be saying to them,—"O death, I will be thy plagues; O grave, I will be thy destruction!" Hos. xiii: 14. Then he conquered Satan, and all the powers of darkness. And ever since then he has gone on conquering. He has never lost a battle. He is always victorious. He succeeds in everything he undertakes to do. His great work in the world is converting and saving souls. And he is wonderfully victorious in carrying on this work. No matter how hard or desperate any case seems, when he takes hold of it, he always succeeds. Look at some illustrations of the victorious working of Jesus.

"The Infidel Converted by a Flower." A gentleman living in Texas was an unbeliever. One day he was walking in his garden reading a book. He read this sentence,—"God works according to the rules of Geometry." He closed the book, and began to think. "I always thought," said he to himself, "that things were made by chance. Is there a rule about every thing?"

Just then he saw close by a sweet little flower, known as the "Texas Star." He picked it up, and began to examine it. He counted the petals. He found there were five. He counted the stamens, there were five of them. He counted the divisions at the base of the flower, there were five of them. Then he examined another flower. It was the same with that. Another and another were examined. It was the same with all. There were five petals, and five stamens, and so on, in every case. "How is this?" he said to himself. "If these flowers were made by chance, some of them would have three petals, and some two, and some

none.   But now they all have five; never more,
and never less.   Here is work done by rule.   If
it is done in this way, there must be some one
to do it.   And who can that be?   O, I see."
And then he picked up the little flower, and
kissed it, and said:—"Bloom on, little flower;
sing on little birds; you have a God, and I have
a God; the God that made these little flowers
made me."

Here is another illustration of the victorious
power of Jesus in winning souls to himself.   We
may call it:

"An Infidel Converted by a Bird."   Some
years ago a gentleman in New York met a
young friend of his who had just returned from
South America.   The young man's father had
left him very rich.   His money had led him
into all sorts of wickedness, and before going
to South America, he had become an open and
avowed infidel.   Now, he was an humble, earnest Christian.   His friend was delighted to find
what a blessed change had taken place in his
views and feelings since they had last met, and
he asked him what it was that had led to this
great change.

"I'll tell you, gladly," said the young man.
"You know, I'm very fond of hunting; and

while in South America, I spent much of my time in that way. One beautiful Sabbath morning I went into the woods in search of game. After awhile, feeling weary with roaming about, I sat down on a log to rest. While seated there, my attention was drawn to a neighboring tree by the cries of a bird, which was fluttering over her nest, apparently in great distress.

"On looking around I soon found the cause of this trouble. I saw a venemous snake creeping towards the tree, with his eye fixed on the bird and her nest. Presently I saw the male bird fly quickly away, as if anxious to get something. In a little while he returned with a twig, covered with leaves, in his mouth. Perching near the nest, he laid the twig very carefully over his mate and her young, entirely covering them, and then, taking his place on one of the topmost branches of the tree, he awaited the arrival of the enemy.

"By this time the snake had reached the spot: twisting himself around the trunk, he climbed up the tree. Then gliding along the branch till he came near the nest, he lifted his head as if he were going to dart upon the poor bird. He looked at the nest for a moment, and then, suddenly throwing back his head, as if he had been shot, he made his way down the tree as fast as he could, and went off.

"I felt very curious to find out the explanation of this strange conduct on the part of the snake; and so, climbing up the tree, and examining the leaves of the twig which had been such a shield and defence to that helpless bird, I found that it had been broken off from a bush which is poisonous to the snake, and which it is never known to touch.

"In a moment the question arose in my mind—Who taught this bird its only weapon of defence in such an hour of danger? And quick as thought came the answer,—None, but God Almighty, that great Being whose very existence I have denied, but in whose pardoning mercy through Jesus Christ, I now find peace, and hope, and joy."

It is this victorious King, who is represented as seated on a white horse, "going forth conquering, and to conquer." Rev. xix: 11; vi: 2. And he will go on conquering, until, as St. Paul tells us, "at the name of Jesus, every knee shall bow, and every tongue confess that Jesus Christ is Lord to the glory of God the Father." Phil. ii: 10, 16.

Well then may Jesus be spoken of as a *victorious king.*

And now, passing on from David to Solomon, there are *two* things about his reign which remind us of Jesus.

*When we think of Jesus as a king like Solomon, we are taught that he was to be—*A WISE—*king.*

We are told that God came to Solomon one night, soon after he had been made king. He told him to ask for anything he would like to have, and it should be given him. Most kings would have asked for great riches, or great honor, or great victories over their enemies. Solomon asked for nothing of this kind, but only for wisdom, that he might be able to govern his people well. This certainly showed that he was a wise king already, or else he would not have asked for such a gift as this.

God was pleased with his prayer, and answered it. He gave him wisdom, greater than any other king ever had. One proof of Solomon's wisdom has come down to us in the books of the Bible that he wrote. These are the book of Proverbs, the book of Ecclesiastes, and the Song of Solomon. His wisdom was so great, that while he was reigning in Jerusalem, the report of him went out through all the world. Our Saviour when on earth, spoke of— "the Queen of the South"—or of Sheba—who "came from the uttermost parts of the earth to hear the wisdom of Solomon." We have an account of this visit in II. Chron. ix: 1-9.

And Solomon reminds us of Jesus in this respect. He is indeed a wise king. There never was any one so wise as he is. St. Paul tells us that—"in him are hid *all the treasures* of wisdom and knowledge." Col. ii: 3. He knows all about everybody and everything. We have an illustration of his wisdom in the wonderful way in which he converts people, and makes them his subjects.

"The Prisoner Converted by a Child."— Some time ago a gentleman was standing on the platform of a railway station in New York. He had a little girl with him about seven years old. As they stood there some policemen came along. They had charge of a prisoner, whose wrists were chained together. He was a fierce, hard-featured, desperate looking fellow, who had committed a great crime. The officers were taking him to the penitentiary, where he was to be kept as a prisoner all the rest of his life.

The gentleman told his little daughter Alice about the man. She felt very much interested in him, and could not keep from looking at him, with her little eyes full of pity. It seemed to annoy the man to be looked at. Alice saw this, and fearing that she had hurt his feelings, she slipped away from her father, and going near the prisoner, she whispered in his ear:

"I didn't mean to plague you, poor man; only I'm sorry for you. And Jesus is sorry for you, too."

No one heard these whispered words except the prisoner and God who hears all things. But they took strong hold of that hardened man's feelings. He could not get rid of them. And the picture of that dear child's face, with her grieved look of tender pity, went with him through all the long ride of that day; and when he passed into his lonely cell, those words, and that picture passed in with him. And they remained with him, producing a strange effect.

He had been in that prison before. The keeper knew him well. He was the most troublesome prisoner they ever had. And now, when he had come back for life, he expected to have nothing but trouble in trying to manage him.

But, to the surprise and wonder of the keeper, from that time on, the prisoner he had dreaded so much, gave him no more trouble. And as time passed on, he grew gentler and more pleasant every day. But the wonder was explained, when as months passed by, and the change continued, the chaplain asked him one day, how it was that he had turned out so different a man from what they expected?

"It is easily explained," said the man. "A child was sorry for me. She told me that Jesus was sorry for me; and her pity and his broke my heart."

Those simple words of that loving child, with the tidings of a Saviour's love, led that hardened sinner to repentance. He became a Christian. Jesus is a wise king, seeing he can convert men in a way so wonderful, and make them his servants.

And then we see what a wise king he is in the way in which he governs those who become his servants. A great many things happen to them which they do not understand at the time; but after waiting awhile, they find that it was all for the best. The Bible tells us that Jesus is "*making all things to work together for good to those who love him.*" Rom. viii: 28. Here is an illustration of the way in which this wise king rules or governs for the good of his people:

"All for the Best." An aged servant of God was travelling in the East. He rode on a donkey,

as is the custom in that country.   At the close
of the day he came to a town where he intended
to spend the night.   The gates were closed and
he could not get in.   Hungry and thirsty, he
·was obliged to pass the night in the open air.
Instead of fretting about it, he said,—"What
God orders is best," and laid himself down to
sleep.   Near him was his faithful donkey.   The
old man had a lighted lantern which he hung
up on the tree under whose spreading branches
he was to rest.   Before long a storm arose, and
put out the light in his lantern.   Then a lion
that was prowling near sprung upon his donkey,
and devoured it.   He awoke, and found himself
alone, and in the dark.   "What God does is
best," was still his saying, as quietly he waited
for the day.

As soon as the morning came, he arose and
went to the town.   The gates were open, for
during the night it had been robbed and plun-
dered.   A band of robbers had attacked it.   They
had killed the inhabitants, or taken them away
prisoners.   And now the good man saw the
meaning of what had happened to him during
the night.   It was well that the storm had put
out the light in his lantern, or it would have
drawn the robbers to him.   And it was well that

His First Miracle at the Marriage of Cana

And the third day there was a marriage in Cana of Galilee; and the mother of Jesus was there. And both Jesus was called, and his disciples, to the marriage. And when they wanted wine, the mother of Jesus saith unto him, They have no wine. And there were set there six waterpots of stone. . . . Jesus saith unto them, Fill the waterpots with water. And they filled them up to the brim. And he saith unto them, Draw out now, and bear unto the governor of the feast. And they bare *it*. When the ruler of the feast had tasted the water that was made wine, and knew not whence it was: (but the servants which drew the water knew;) the governor of the feast called the bridegroom. And saith unto him, Every man at the beginning doth set forth good wine; and when men have well drunk, then that which is worse: *but* thou hast kept the good wine until now. This beginning of miracles did Jesus in Cana of Galilee.—*St. John ii: 1–3, 6–11.*

NOTE BY THE ARTIST

The typical Syrian house of the better class, which has been selected for this painting, partly surrounds the central quadrangle, the other two sides of which are guarded by high walls. Two women, grinding at the mill, are seated in the flickering shade of an almond tree, at the entrance of the kitchen, which with other offices occupies the basement of the dwelling; while servants bearing dishes for the feast ascend by an outside stair to the guest chamber or "large upper room." A carrier replenishes the jars from the goat skin bag or "bottle" in which he has brought water from the public cistern.

19

19

the lion had killed his donkey, for by its loud braying it might have caused the death of its master. And so with a grateful heart, he said to himself,—"How true it is that what God does is best!"

Like Solomon, Jesus is a *wise* king.

And lastly, when we think of Jesus as a king like Solomon, we see that he was to be—a PEACEFUL —*king.*

Solomon had no bear or lion to go after, and no giant to fight, as was the case with his father. David fought many battles, but Solomon never fought one. His reign was a prosperous and peaceful one. When he was comparing his own reign with that of his father's, he said,—"David, my father had wars about him on every side; but God hath given me rest on every side, so that there is neither adversary, nor evil occurrent." I. Kings v: 3, 4. And when we think of Solomon, in his peaceful reign, it reminds us of Jesus. He is indeed a *peaceful* king. He is called—*"The Prince of Peace."* When the angels appeared to the shepherds of Bethlehem, to sing their glad song over the birth of Jesus, *"Peace on Earth"* was what they loved to sing about. The gospel of Jesus is "the gospel of peace." The kingdom of Jesus, when established in our world, will be—a kingdom of peace.

Everything connected with this kingdom will be so peaceful that the prophet Isaiah tells us even the wild animals will lose their fierceness, and live in peace with each other. In describing that peaceful kingdom, these are the words that he uses:—"The wolf also shall dwell with the lamb, and the leopard shall lie down with the kid; and the calf and the young lion and the fatling together; and a little child shall lead them. And the cow and the bear shall feed; their young ones shall lie down together; and the lion shall eat straw,"—or hay—"like the ox." Is. xi: 6, 7.

And the followers of Jesus are expected to be like him. They must have the same mind or spirit that was in him. They must be peace-loving, and peace-making people. The rule by which they must live and walk is that given in Rom. xii: 18:—"If it be possible, as much as lieth in *you*, live peaceably with all men." What a blessed thing it will be for our world when all the people who live in it shall, as the apostle says,—"follow after the things which make for peace." Rom. xiv: 19. Here is a striking illustration, from a converted heathen, to show how far the grace of God will go in overcoming the strongest passions of men and teaching them to follow out the peace-loving spirit of the gospel of Jesus. We may call it:

"Revenge Overcome; or, Grace Conquering." —An English missionary in New Zealand was about to leave his work there, for awhile, and make a visit to England. On the Sunday before leaving, he held a service, at which were present all who had been brought to a knowledge of Christ through his ministry. The church was filled with hundreds of the New Zealanders. After the sermon was over the Lord's Supper was administered. The first rail was filled, when the missionary, Mr. Taylor, saw a man who was kneeling at one end of the chancel, suddenly get up—before receiving the bread and wine— walk down the whole length of the church and take his seat. While the missionary was wondering what this meant, and before he had recovered from his surprise, the man returned, knelt down in the same place, and received the communion.

The man's manner in doing this was so strange, that, after the service was over, Mr. Taylor spoke to him about it, and asked him why he had disturbed the whole congregation in that way.

This was his answer:—"Mr. Taylor, when I went up to receive the communion, I did not know at whose side I should be kneeling. Judge of my surprise and horror, when I found that the man kneeling next to me was the very man, who, a few years before, had murdered my father, and drank his blood. You know how very strong the feeling of blood revenge is among the New Zealanders. I was a heathen then, and I swore, by my gods, that I would murder that man the first time I saw him. I had never seen him since then, till we met at the chancel rail. You may imagine how I felt when I found him kneeling by my side. I could not stand it. It overpowered me. I rose and walked away from the chancel. While doing this I seemed to see that upper room in Jerusalem where this supper was instituted. I seemed to hear a voice say,—'By this shall all men know that ye are my disciples, if ye have love one to another.' But I was not willing to go back. I sat down in my seat. Then another scene seemed to pass before my mind. I thought I saw my Saviour hanging on the cross. His head was bowed. The blood was dropping from his wounds. I seemed to hear his prayer for his murderers,—'Father, forgive them, for they know not what they do.' Then I went back, and kneeled down beside the man whose hands had once been red with the blood of my father. But my revenge was overcome. The grace of God had turned my enmity into love." This man was a true servant of Jesus, the peaceful King. Let us all seek to have the same spirit. Then we shall be children of peace.

Thus we have spoken of Jesus as the king like David and Solomon. This sets him before us as a *chosen* king—a *prepared* king—a *victorious* king—a *wise* king—a *peaceful* king.

JONAH AND JESUS CONTRASTED AND COMPARED

THE history of Jonah is very interesting and instructive. It shows us clearly, as St. Paul says, that "whatsoever things were written aforetime," in the Old Testament, "were written for our learning." Rom. xv: 4. The histories written there, both of the persons who lived then and of the things they did, were all intended to give us instructions about the character and work of the *Great Saviour*, who was to appear in the fulness of time, that he might die for our sins, and "open the kingdom of heaven to all believers."

But we should never have thought of looking for any figure or type of Christ in the history of Jonah, if our blessed Lord himself, had not taught us to do so. He has done this, however. He has spoken so clearly and plainly of Jonah, and of certain things in his history, as intended to teach us about himself, that we need not hesitate a moment to make this use of them. The things written in the history of Jonah were intended to teach us valuable lessons respecting Christ. Here is another of those Old Testament *shadows* that are thrown across our path, on purpose to point us to Jesus.

There is no part of the Old Testament history to which so much objection has been made, and with which so much fault has been found, as this of Jonah. Some people think that the story of Jonah and the great fish is so strange that it cannot be true. But our Saviour knew whether it was true, or not, when he was on earth. If it had not been true, he would not have spoken of it as he did. The way in which he spoke of it, proves that it *is* true. If we believe what the Bible tells about Jesus, we must believe what the Bible tells us about Jonah. *Jesus endorsed Jonah.* We are just as sure, therefore, that the history of Jonah is a true history as we are sure that two and two make four, or as we are sure that the sun rises in the East, and sets in the West. And so, while we are speaking of the types and figures of the Old Testament we must not leave Jonah out. We find a shadow here that points us to Jesus.

There are some things in Jonah's history and character, very unlike anything we find in the history and character of Jesus. But there are some things in Jonah in which he was like Jesus. Now, when we set the points of difference between two things opposite to each other, we call it a *contrast*. And when we speak of the points in which two things are alike, we call it a *comparison*. We have to do both of these things in this case. And so, our present subject may be thus stated:

"JONAH AND JESUS CONTRASTED AND COMPARED."

The contrast between Jonah and Jesus, takes in *three* things; and the comparison between them, takes in *two* things.

When we think of Jonah as a preacher, the first point of contrast between him and Jesus is that he was an—UNWILLING—*preacher.*

Jonah lived about eight hundred or eight hundred and fifty years before Christ. He was one of the earlier of the Old Testament prophets. We find the book that bears his name near the middle of what are called the twelve minor prophets. If it were placed in our Bibles just where it belongs in the order of time, then it would appear before the prophecies of

Isaiah. Jonah lived about the same time that Elijah and Elisha did. The Jews say that he was the son of that good widow woman at Zarephath, with whom Elijah made his home during the latter part of the great famine sent upon the land in the days of King Ahab. If this were so, then Jonah owed his life to the prayers of Elijah, the man of God.

We know little about this prophet, except what we read of him in the book that bears his name. This book begins without any introduction, by telling us of a particular work that God wished Jonah to do. He was commanded to go to Nineveh, and preach to the people there about their sins.

This city was one of the oldest in the world. The first time we find it mentioned in the Bible is in Gen. x: 9-12. Nimrod, "the mighty hunter," spoken of in that chapter, is supposed to have been the founder of it. It was beautifully situated on the banks of the river Tigris, in the land of Assyria. At the time when Jonah was sent to Nineveh to preach, it was more than a thousand years old. What a grand old city it must have been! And it is in connection with this famous city that we find out what an *unwilling* prophet Jonah was. Nineveh was a very wicked city. The people who lived in it were all idolaters. It would seem as if, in some way or other, they had become more wicked than usual about this time. They had provoked God to anger by their sins. He told Jonah to go there and preach to the people about their wickedness. But, strange as it appears, Jonah was not willing to go.

We are not told what was the reason of this unwillingness. It might have been that he thought they would not listen to him; or it might have been that he was afraid they would be angry with him and kill him; or it might have been because they were Gentiles and he was a Jew. The Jews were what we should call very narrow-minded on this subject. They thought that God did not love, or care, for the people of any other nation than theirs. They could not bear to hear any one express an opinion different from this. When our Saviour was on earth, he was preaching one day in the synagogue to the people of the city of Nazareth, where he had been brought up. In the course of his sermon he mentioned one or two instances in which God had shown kindness to some people who were not of their nation. But they would not hear him. It made them so angry that they broke up the meeting, and even tried to kill him.   You can see the account of it in Luke iv: 16-30.   And the same thing happened to St. Paul.   He was making a speech to his countrymen, the Jews in the city of Jerusalem.   He told them all about his wonderful conversion; and they listened very attentively to what he was saying till he mentioned that God had told him to go and preach the gospel to the Gentiles.   Then they would listen no longer, but cried out,—"Away with such a fellow from the earth, for it is not fit that he should live."   Acts xxii: 22.   And this may have been the reason why Jonah was unwilling to go and preach to the men of Nineveh.   But, whatever the reason, certain it is that Jonah was unwilling to go.   In the first chapter of Jonah, and the third verse, we are told that, "he arose and fled to Tarshish, from the presence of the Lord." He went down to Joppa, now called Jaffa, which was a city on the coast of the Mediterranean Sea, about thirty miles from Jerusalem.   Here he found a ship going to Tarshish, and took his passage on board of her.

We do not know exactly where Tarshish was. Some suppose it was the city of Tartessus in Spain: others think it was the city of Tarsus, on the coast of Asia Minor, which was the birth-place of St. Paul.   How strange it was that one of God's prophets should have supposed that by taking a sea-voyage, he could get away from "the presence of the Lord!"   Did he not know that God was in every place?   Had he never read what David said in Ps. cxxxix: 7-12?

"Whither shall I go from thy spirit? or whither shall I flee from thy presence?

"If I ascend up into heaven, thou art there: if I make my bed in hell, behold, thou art there.

"If I take the wings of the morning, and dwell in the uttermost parts of the sea; even there shall thy hand lead me, and thy right hand shall hold me.

"If I say, Surely the darkness shall cover me; even the night shall be light about me.

"Yea, the darkness hideth not from thee; but the night shineth as the day; the darkness and the light are both alike to thee."

Here, then we see Jonah as an *unwilling* prophet or preacher.

And how unlike Jesus he was in this respect! What a contrast between Jonah and Jesus we have here!   When God wanted Jesus to come down from heaven and preach to men about their sins, he was perfectly willing to come.   We

have the very words that he spoke about it, in
the fortieth Psalm, verses seven and eight. "Lo!
I come to do thy will, O, my God. I *delight* to
do it." Jonah would have had nothing to suffer
if he had gone to Nineveh to do what God told
him; but still he was unwilling to go. Jesus
had much to suffer when he came to do God's
will. He knew all about this suffering before
he came; and yet he was willing to come. Here
was a great contrast between Jonah and Jesus.

*But the next point in this contrast is seen when
we remember that Jonah was—*A SUCCESSFUL—
preacher.

What happened to Jonah during the voyage
that he took from Joppa we shall see by and by.
God taught him a lesson before that voyage was
ended which he never forgot. He learned that
lesson well, and it had a good effect upon him.
It took away all his unwillingness to obey God.
And when he had taught him this lesson, God
said to Jonah again,—"Arise, go to Nineveh,
that great city, and preach unto it, the preaching that I bid thee." Jonah iii: 2. And he went.
And here we are told that, "Nineveh was an
exceeding great city of three days' journey."
This means that it would take a person three
days to walk round it. A day's journey, for a

Jesus Purgeth the Temple

And the Jews passover was at hand, and Jesus went up to Jerusalem. And found in the temple those that sold oxen and sheep and doves, and the changers of money sitting. And when he had made a scourge of small cords, he drove them all out of the temple, and the sheep, and the oxen; and poured out the changers' money, and overthrew the tables. And said unto them that sold doves, Take these things hence; make not my Father's house an house of merchandise. And his disciples remembered that it was written, The zeal of thine house hath eaten me up.—*St. John ii: 13–17.*

NOTE BY THE ARTIST

Well indeed might Jesus stigmatize the chief priests of the Temple as hypocrites; for while these men were sticklers for such minor details of purification as the cleansing of cup and platter, they sanctioned, for the sake of gain derived, from the rents of cattle-pens and shops, and from the sale of pigeons, the scandalous desecration of God's House by the filth and traffic of the great annual fair. This, though held certainly in the outer, or Court of the Heathen, to which all had access, must nevertheless, by its accompanying sights and noise and evil odors, have caused unseemly interruption and distraction to those worshippers who were intent upon the solemn services of the adjacent sanctuary. The reform inaugurated by Jesus on this occasion seems to have had certain definite, though but transient, results. Rules of almost unnecessary strictness were formulated and for a time enforced; but long-established custom, convenience, and greed, speedily combined to make such rules a dead letter, and, as we learn from the subsequent narrative, the condition of matters was within three years as bad as ever.

person travelling on foot is about twenty miles. And, at this rate, Nineveh must have been about twenty miles in length or breadth, and about sixty miles in circumference. We are told that there were in Nineveh, at this time, "six score thousand persons who could not discern between their right hand and their left." Ch. iv: 11. This means that there were a hundred and twenty thousand children in it, who were not more than three or four years old. Now, in a large city, for every child of this age, it is safe to reckon that there are at least five persons who are older. And if we multiply a hundred and twenty thousand by five, it gives us six hundred thousand as the number of the inhabitants of Nineveh, at the time of Jonah's visit there.

A modern city of six hundred thousand inhabitants would not cover as much ground as Nineveh covered. London, the largest city in the world, has a population more than five times as great as that of Nineveh, and yet it does not cover nearly as much ground as that ancient city did. But it is easy enough to account for this difference. For the houses in Nineveh were not so crowded together as they are in London and New York, and most of our modern cities. In those eastern cities they had beautiful gardens and large cultivated fields between many of the houses, and in this way the great space here spoken of would easily be filled up.

But Nineveh was not only a great city as to its size, it was great also as to its *beauty*. We have no description of the appearance it presented when Jonah saw it. But lately a great deal has been found out about this old city, so that we can form a very good idea of how it looked at that time.

About two hundred years after Jonah's death, Nineveh was taken and destroyed. This destruction was most thorough and complete. The inhabitants were all either destroyed or taken away. Neither man, nor woman, nor child was left to live there. The great temples and splendid palaces of Nineveh were entirely overthrown. And in foretelling the destruction of this famous city, the prophet Nahum makes use of two very remarkable expressions: one was that "her palaces should be *dissolved*." Ch. ii: 6. The other is in Ch. i: 14, where God says of this city,—"I will *make thy grave*, for thou art vile." Now we might talk about *destroying* our public buildings, but we never should talk of *dissolving* them. There is our capitol at Washington, made of white marble. We can easily understand how it might be destroyed, but we cannot understand how it could be *dissolved*. But it is very easy to see how this could happen to Nineveh. Her temples and palaces had their foundations and lower stories built of stone, at least they were covered or faced with slabs of stone. But the upper parts of all those buildings were made of sun-dried bricks. When these were thrown down, and exposed to the influence of the weather, they would crumble, or turn to dust or clay. As the prophet said they would "*be dissolved.*" And so the upper parts of those great buildings would crumble, and bury up the lower portions of them that were made of stone. The prophet said that Nineveh should be buried. And this was just what happened to it. And so completely was it buried, and covered up by its own ruins, that for long centuries no trace of Nineveh had ever been seen. Nobody knew just where the city had stood. Indeed, some men who professed not to believe the Bible went so far as to say that there never had been such a city as Nineveh, and that what the Bible said about it was not true.

But no one can say this any longer; for within a few years past the ruins of Nineveh have been discovered. By digging down into the great heaps and mounds spread over the plains, near the river Tigris, very wonderful things have been found out. The remains of splendid temples, and palaces, and other buildings, have been uncovered. These are spread out over miles and miles of the surrounding country. The walls of many of these buildings are lined with great slabs of stone. These slabs are filled with sculptured figures. Here are found huge winged lions and bulls. There are also representations of sieges and battle-scenes. The names and figures of kings mentioned in the Bible are found here. The name of Hezekiah, king of Judah, has been found among these ruins. And not only the name, but the figure of Sennacherib, the Assyrian king, mentioned in the Bible has also been found. It is cut in stone, larger than life, and represents him as sitting on his throne and holding a sceptre in his hand.

Great numbers of these stone slabs have been dug out from the ruins, carried over to England, and put in the British Museum in London. After examining the foundations of one of these ruined palaces, an English architect has made a drawing of what he supposes was the appearance which it presented at the time when Jonah visited Nineveh. As Jonah drew nigh, he saw the walls of the city rising up a hundred feet high. Along on the walls were fifteen hundred towers, each rising to the height of two hundred feet. And then, as he looked through the gates he would see those splendid buildings. How grand it must have appeared!

And now Jonah enters the gate of the city. He is a total stranger to the men of Nineveh. He makes his way along the broad avenues that lead through the city. Here and there, in front of its great palaces—in the market places, and wherever the people meet together—he pauses, and delivers his solemn message:—*"Yet forty days, and Nineveh shall be destroyed."* Through all the length and breadth of the great city those startling words are ringing. The people are wonderfully aroused. They meet in crowds, and talk about the strange preacher, and his message. A wonderful spell seems to come over them. They listen with awe. No one mocks or trifles. The report of the Jewish prophet and his message spreads through the city. The king hears of it in his palace. It has the same effect on him. He proclaims a fast. All the people, from the highest to the lowest, spend three days in fasting and prayer. They entreat God to pardon their sins, and turn from his anger. Their prayers were heard, and answered, and Nineveh was spared.

And here we see how wonderfully successful Jonah was as a prophet, or preacher. There never was anything like it. Why, even our blessed Lord himself, was not so successful in preaching as Jonah was. He felt this, and spoke of it when he was on earth. He said to the Jews, one day,—"The men of Nineveh shall rise in judgment with this generation, and condemn it, for they repented at the preaching of Jonah, and behold a greater than Jonah is here." Matt. xii: 41. Here Jesus makes this very point of contrast that we are making between himself and Jonah. "A greater than Jonah," indeed he was, and yet, in preaching, Jonah was more successful than he. Think of the *person* of Jesus. How full of perfection he was! Then think of the person of Jonah. How full of *im*-perfection he was. Yet Jonah was more successful than Jesus in preaching. Think of the *words* of Jesus. They were gracious words, full of wisdom, and love, and tenderness. Then think of the words of Jonah. They told of nothing but the anger of God. Yet Jonah was more successful than Jesus in preaching. Think of the *works* of Jesus. How many miracles he performed! Jonah did not perform one miracle. And yet this point of contrast remains. Notwithstanding all these things, Jonah was more successful as a preacher than Jesus was.

But there is another point of contrast between Jonah and Jesus, and this is that Jonah was— A SELFISH—*preacher.*

When Jonah had finished his preaching at Nineveh, he waited awhile under the shade of the gourd which God had caused to grow for him, to see if God was going to destroy the city, as he had threatened to do. But when he found that, on account of the repentance of the people of Nineveh, God had pardoned their sins and was not going to destroy them, he was very much displeased, and wanted to die. How strange it was that a good man should have given way to such wrong feelings! Yet, *this* is just what Jonah did.

We have often heard of ministers who were distressed and troubled because they were *not* successful in leading men to repentance through their preaching. But in Jonah we have an example—the only one ever known—of a preacher distressed and troubled because he *was* successful in leading men to repentance by his preaching. You may ask how we can account for this? Why, it seems Jonah was afraid that if Nineveh was not destroyed, as he had said it would be, people would think he was not a true prophet. This is the most natural explanation of Jonah's feelings about this matter that can be given. And if this was the real secret of his trouble, then, we see clearly that he cared more for *his own* honor and glory than he did for the honor and glory of God. This shows us how selfish Jonah was. And what a contrast there was between Jonah and Jesus here! Think of Jonah fretting, and worrying, and wishing to die, because the people of Nineveh had repented under his preaching, and been forgiven, and so had been saved from destruction. And then think of Jesus weeping over the people of Jerusalem, because they *would not* repent and be saved. Think of his tender, touching lamentation, as "he beheld the city, and wept over it, saying, *Oh, Jerusalem! Jerusalem! how often would I have gathered thy children together, as a hen gathereth her chickens under her wings, and ye would not!*" Jonah thought only about his own glory; but Jesus thought only about the glory of his Father. It was this feeling which led him to offer the prayer—"Father, glorify thy name." John xii: 28. *This* was always the strongest feeling with him. *This* was what he always desired, and longed for above everything else. Jonah was a selfish prophet, but, in Jesus there was no selfishness.

Thus we have looked at the *contrast* between Jonah and Jesus, or the things in which they *differed* from each other. Now let us look at the *comparison* between them, or the things in which they were alike.

Jonah was—READY TO DIE FOR THE SAKE OF OTHERS,—*and in this he was like Jesus.*

A terrible storm overtook the ship in which Jonah sailed from Joppa. It was so severe as to threaten the destruction of the ship. The sailors called on their heathen gods, but the storm grew worse. They threw some of the cargo overboard to lighten the ship, yet all the while the storm increased. When they found it growing more and more furious, they made up their minds that it must have been sent on account of the wickedness committed by some one on board. They cast lots to find whether it was one of the crew, or the passenger, Jonah, who was guilty. The lot fell on Jonah. They asked him what he had done. He told them frankly who he was, and what he had done. Then they were more afraid than ever. They asked Jonah what they should do. He told them to throw him overboard, as he knew the storm had been sent on his account. And this brings out the point that we are now speaking of. It shows that Jonah was *ready to die for the sake of others*. He might have refused to let them throw him into the sea. He might have said:—"You shall not throw me overboard. I have as much right to live as anybody. I shall cling to the ship, just as long as she remains afloat." But he did not say any such thing. He knew the storm had come on his account. He expected it would cease at once when he was out of the way. And so he was ready to die for the sake of others. We do not see many goods things in Jonah's character; but this was one, and we are glad to speak of it.

Jonah was a figure of Christ in his readiness to die for others. True, he was but a feeble figure of Christ in this respect. The comparison is not very striking here. Christ's readiness to die for us was much greater than the readiness of Jonah to die for the sake of his shipmates. Jonah was ready to die when he could not very well help it. It seemed as if he was compelled to die. But Jesus was willing to die when he was not obliged to do so. He offered freely to die in our stead.

And then again the persons for whom Jonah was ready to die, were his companions, his shipmates, his friends; but Christ died for "the ungodly"—Rom. v: 6—for his "enemies"—Rom. v: 8. This was wonderful indeed. Nothing that ever happened in all the world was half so wonderful as this. We see how true it is, as Jesus said that—"*a greater than Jonah is here.*" In his readiness to die for others, he was greater than Jonah. In his love for his enemies he was greater than Jonah. One thing in which Jonah was like Jesus was in his readiness to die for others.

And then there was another thing in which Jonah was like Jesus, this was—THE LENGTH OF TIME THAT HE WAS BURIED.

This was the point of comparison between Jonah and himself that our Saviour especially referred to. He said, when he was on earth, that—"as Jonah was three days and three nights in the fish's belly, so the Son of man should be three days and three nights in the heart of the earth." Matt. xii: 40. This is the part of Jonah's history that has been the most found fault with. Yet Jesus takes particular pains to assure us that this part is true. *If we do not believe what the Bible tells us about Jonah, we cannot believe what it tells us about Jesus.*

What we read in the history of Jonah is this:—Ch. i: 14-17—that the sailors tried for a long time to save the ship, without throwing him into the sea; but they found it was impossible. They must either do this, or they would all be lost. Then they prayed to God, and asked him to pardon them for what they were going to do; after this they threw Jonah into the foaming waters. Immediately the storm ceased; and the sea became calm again. But what became of Jonah? We are told that "the Lord had prepared a great fish to swallow up Jonah." Here you see, it does not say "a whale," but "a great fish." We do find the word whale in our English New Testament, when it tells us what Jesus said about Jonah. But then remember that Jesus did not speak in English, but in Greek; and the Greek word that Jesus used here does not mean a whale, but a great fish. It was "a great fish" which "God had prepared" for this occasion. It would have been very easy for God to have made a great fish, on purpose to be the living grave of Jonah for the time here spoken of. But it was not necessary for him to do so. There were fish enough in the sea that could have swallowed a man without hurting him, and then have thrown him up alive.

There is a large white shark in the Mediterranean sea which has been known to swallow a man alive, and whole. Müller, a well-known natural historian, of good character, relates an incident that illustrates this part of our subject very well:

An English man-of-war was lying at anchor in one of the ports of the Mediterranean. While doing some work on the sides of the ship, one of the sailors fell overboard. Before he could be taken out of the water a shark swallowed him, and he disappeared. The captain ordered a gun to be fired at the fish. The ball struck it, and it vomited up the sailor. He was picked up by his comrades alive, and very little hurt. The sailors followed up the shark, caught it, and killed it. It was twenty feet in length, and weighed nearly four thousand pounds. Sharks have been found in this sea as much as sixty feet in length. The sailor, who had been swallowed by this fish, took its skin off carefully, had it stuffed, carried it home to England, and exhibited it as a show to illustrate the Bible story of Jonah and the great fish.

That "great fish" of which the Bible speaks, became, as it were, the tomb, or grave, or burial place of Jonah. He remained in that fish exactly the same length of time that Jesus was buried in that rocky tomb near Jerusalem. And this was just the point of the comparison that Jesus made between Jonah and himself. He said, "As Jonah was three days and three nights in the fish's belly, so should the Son of man be three days and three nights in the heart of the earth." Matt. xii: 40. This does not mean exactly three whole days and three whole nights, according to our way of speaking. When we wish to speak of the twenty-four hours which make up a whole day and a whole night, we can only do it by using three separate words. We have to say, day and night. But the Jews and the Greeks had one word which expressed the time denoted by the three words just spoken of. It was a word of four syllables, and was made by putting together the Greek word for day and for night. They called this time a nuk-tha-me-ron. And then they called any part of a day, or any part of a night, a nuk-tha-me-ron. So that if they wished to speak of the whole day, or one whole night, and two parts of a day and night, they would apply this same word to each, and call them three nuk-tha-me-rons, or three days and nights. The Jews reckoned their day and night from six o'clock in the evening of one day to six o'clock in the evening of the next day. And so if the fish swallowed Jonah, say about three o'clock on Friday afternoon, and he remained in the fish till some time on Sunday morning, we can see how that would make, according to the Jewish way of reckoning, three days and three nights. From three o'clock on Friday afternoon to six o'clock in the evening would make part of the Friday, or the first day and night. From six o'clock on Friday evening to six o'clock on Saturday evening would make the whole of the Saturday, or second day and night; while from six o'clock on Saturday evening to any time on Sunday morning would make part of the Sunday, or the third day and night. And so we see that as the Jews counted time, Jonah was in the fish three days and three nights, and this was just the length of time during which our Saviour lay buried in the grave. And so the comparison here is complete. Jonah and Jesus were alike in the *length of time they were buried.*

We have spoken of three points of contrast between Jonah and Jesus, or three things in which Jonah was very unlike Jesus. He was an *unwilling* preacher—a *successful* preacher—a *selfish* preacher. We have also spoken of two points of comparison between Jonah and Jesus, or two things in which they were like each other:—*They were both ready to die for others;* and *they were both buried for the same length of time.*

And when we think of the wonderful love of Jesus in being willing to lie down in the grave for us, it should lead us to love him with all our hearts, and make us willing to go anywhere and do anything to show our love for him. Let me close with two illustrations. One shows what effect the thought of God's love had on a little child; the other shows what effect it had upon a minister of the gospel:

A Christian mother had been talking one day to her little boy, three years old, about the love of God in sending his Son into the world to die for us. It seemed to touch the little fellow's heart very much. By and by, while still thinking of what his mother had taught him; she saw him all alone by himself, kissing his little hand and waving it up towards the sky.

"What are you doing, Birdie?" asked his mother. "I 'tans up and tisses Dod," was his sweet reply. It was a childlike, but beautiful illustration of the text,—"*We love him because he first loved us.*" So the thought of Christ's love should lead us all to love him.

The other story may be called "The Minister in the Robber's Vault." This incident I am about to tell occurred many years ago in Edinburgh, during the time when the cholera was prevailing there fearfully. A minister of the gospel had been out nearly all day visiting the sick and dying, and burying the dead. He went home feeling weary and worn. When he went to bed he could not sleep, for thinking of the many sad and sorrowful scenes he had witnessed during the day. He lay tossing in his bed till midnight. Then there came a loud ring at his door-bell. The servant went to the door, and came back to say that a man there was very anxious to see him. He dressed himself and went down. He held up the light to get a good view of the man; but it was not encouraging. His face was covered with a thick, shaggy beard, and he looked very much like a robber.

"What do you want with me?" asked the minister.

"I want you to come and visit a dying man who wishes very much to see you."

"What is his complaint?"

"Cholera."

The minister hesitated about going. The man saw it, and said,—"Don't be afraid, sir. Leave your watch and money behind, you'll be safe."

He resolved to go. But before starting he went back to his room, and kneeling down in prayer, asked God to take care of him, and keep him from harm.

Then he went with the strange man. He led him a long way through the town. At last they came to a lonely place in the outskirts. Here the man stopped, took out a jack-knife and scraped away some dirt from the ground. Presently he opened a trap-door which led into a deep, dark vault. The minister felt afraid at the idea of going down into such a place as that. "Don't be afraid, sir," said the man. Then he let himself down by a rope. On reaching the bottom, he lighted a candle, and setting a ladder up to the mouth of the vault, asked the minister to come down. Again he lifted up his heart in silent prayer to God for his protection, and went down the ladder. As he reached the bottom he felt like Daniel in the den of lions. Gazing round in the dim light he saw a number of savage looking men lying about in different positions. That gloomy vault was the retreat of a band of robbers. The man led the minister to the further end of the vault. There, on a bed of straw, lay a man dying of cholera. Sitting down on a stool by his side, he said to the dying man:

"Did you wish to see me, my friend?"

"I did," he replied, in a clear, decided voice.

"Why do you wish to see me?"

"Because," said the man, "some time ago I wandered into your church and heard you read some words that I have never been able to forget. I wish to hear them again before I die. I thought I could hide myself from God. But he has found me out, and laid his hand upon me. O, God! I have sinned against thee; thou art just; can there be any hope for a wretch like me?" and his whole frame shook with his deep feeling.

"Can you tell any of the words that will bring the passage to my memory?"

"Oh! it was something about God knowing my down-sitting, and mine uprising, and understanding my thoughts and my words."

Then the minister knew it was the one hundred and thirty-ninth Psalm. He took out his Bible and read that Psalm. "Oh! that is it, that is it," said the man in a low voice; "thank God I have heard it again."

Then the minister said,—"The blood of Jesus Christ cleanseth from all sin. This is a faithful saying, and worthy of all acceptation, that Christ Jesus came into the world to save sinners."

"To save sinners," said he; "but, oh! not such a sinner as I have been."

"Yes, such as you are. Hear what God says: —'Come, now, and let us reason together; though your sins be as scarlet, they shall be as white as snow; though they be red like crimson, they shall be as wool.'"

"But, how? O, how?" eagerly asked the dying man. "What must I do to be saved?"

"'Believe on the Lord Jesus Christ, and thou shalt be saved;' your past sins will not condemn you. Christ 'is able to save unto the uttermost all that come unto God through him.'"

The man stretched out his clasped hands, and with his eyes raised towards heaven, exclaimed —"God be merciful to me a sinner," and with that prayer upon his lips he died.

The minister spoke a few earnest, solemn words to the companions of the dead man; and then the man who had brought him there, led him out of the vault, and back towards his home. How thankful that minister felt that God had made him willing to go, as soon as he was sent for, that he might preach the gospel to that poor dying sinner!

And when we think of Jesus, how different he was from Jonah; when we think of the love that made him willing to leave heaven; to come into our dark world; to march on to the cross; to die there, and then to lie down in the grave, in order that we might be saved, how we should love him! and how ready we should be to go anywhere, and do anything that he wishes us to do, that we may show our love for him! We ought to love him because he first loved us. And when we remember the greatness of his love, we may well say for ourselves individually:

> " Were the whole realm of nature mine,
>   *That* were a tribute far too small;
> Love so amazing, so divine,
>   Demands my life, my soul, my all."